New **Head~~~**

Academic Skills
Reading, Writing, and Study Skills

LEVEL 1 **Student's Book**

Richard Harrison
Series Editors: Liz and John Soars

OXFORD

CONTENTS

1 Student life

READING SKILLS Ways of reading
WRITING SKILLS Punctuation (1) • Linking ideas (1) • Checking your writing • Writing about people
VOCABULARY DEVELOPMENT Parts of speech • A dictionary entry (1) • Recording vocabulary (1)

READING How do you read?

1 What kind of reader are you? Complete the quiz. Discuss your answers with a partner.

The reading quiz

1 I like to read …
   a at a desk or table
   b in a comfortable place
   c on a journey
   d anywhere

2 I … read slowly and carefully.
   a always
   b usually
   c sometimes
   d never

3 When I read something in English, …
   a I check every new word in a dictionary.
   b I check a few of the new words.
   c I just read and try to understand.
   d I only look at the pictures and the headings.

2 Look at the words in the box. Do we usually read these things slowly or quickly? Complete the table and compare answers with a partner.

| newspaper   poem   textbook   novel   magazine |
| report   telephone directory   definition |

read quickly	read slowly

3 Read the magazine article *How do you read?* Compare your lists in exercise 2 with the information in the article.

How do you read?

People read in many different places, for example in a park, on a bus, or in a car. This is because books, newspapers, magazines, and so on, are easy to carry. We also read in many different ways, and at different speeds.

Sometimes we read quickly. We just want to get the general idea from a newspaper article, a report, or a book in a bookshop. Perhaps we want to know what it is about, or if it is interesting or important. We call this type of reading 'skimming'. We also read quickly to get a particular piece of information, such as a date, a telephone number, or the name of a restaurant. This is called 'scanning'. We scan timetables, telephone directories, dictionaries, and web pages.

At other times we need to read more carefully. For example, we read a textbook, an article, or a report to understand everything. This is called 'intensive reading' or 'study reading'. Then we read slowly and check the meaning. We use our dictionaries a lot to help us. Perhaps we take notes and try to remember things. Sometimes we need to learn things by heart, for example a poem, or a mathematical equation.

4 Read Study Skill Match situations 1–3 with the ways of reading a–c.

STUDY SKILL Ways of reading

A good reader reads in different ways.
Sometimes you read **slowly and carefully** (*intensive reading / study reading*).
At other times you read **quickly** for the **general idea** (*skimming*) or for **information** (*scanning*).
A good reader chooses the right way to read.

situations	ways of reading
1 ☐ reading a chapter of a physics textbook to understand a topic	a study reading
2 ☐ looking for a room number on an exam timetable	b skimming
3 ☐ choosing an interesting book to read	c scanning

WRITING Describing people

1 **Read Study Skill** Match rules a–f from the Study Skill box with different uses of capital letters 1–6 in the sentences.

STUDY SKILL Punctuation (1)

Use **capital letters** for the first letter of:

a the first word in a sentence, for example: *He studies English.*
b people's names: *Nora*
c titles: *Mr, Mrs, Miss, Dr, Professor*
d cities and countries: *Turkey, Beijing*
e languages: *English*
f the names of schools, colleges, companies: *International College, Microsoft*

Remember – Use a full stop at the end of a sentence, and use a question mark (*?*) at the end of a question.

---

[1] [2]
My name's Victor and I'm a student at the University of Oporto, in Portugal.
I am studying French, Russian, and English because I like languages.
[3]
[4] [5]
Dr Afzal Ahmed is 36 years old. He is a doctor, and he comes from a small
town near Madras, in the south of India.
[6]

2 Rewrite the pairs of sentences. Add capital letters, and full stops or question marks.

1 my name is emin alpay i am a teacher at the middle east technical university in ankara
2 i am a receptionist in a big hotel in singapore the name of the hotel is the royal palace
3 my husband is called sami and he is a pilot he works for air new zealand
4 mrs elly hollemans is a teacher she comes from holland and she teaches german
5 where is the faculty for oriental studies is it in oxford

3 What are texts 1 and 2 about? Skim them to get a general idea.

1

My name is **Mona Saeed** and I am from Manama. It is the capital city of Bahrain. I am a student at Bahrain Training Institute. I am studying computer programming. I hope to work in a bank one day. I am 18 years old and I am single. I have two brothers and three sisters. We all live with our parents and grandmother in a large house in the suburbs of Manama. I speak Arabic, and English quite well. I also understand Farsi, but I can't speak it very well. In my free time I like reading novels, watching TV, and playing computer games.

2

Dr Lee is Chinese and comes from Shanghai, in China. He teaches mathematics and computing at Kuala Lumpur University. He is an Assistant Professor in the Faculty of Science. He is a graduate of Shanghai University and has a PhD from the USA. Dr Lee speaks many languages. As well as Chinese, he speaks very good English, French, and Malay. He is 35 years old and he is married with two children. They live in a small flat on the university campus. He likes music very much and he is an excellent pianist. Dr Lee likes teaching at the university, but in the future he wants to return to China to continue his research.

4 Scan the texts on page 6 to complete the table with information about Mona Saeed and Dr Lee.

	Mona Saeed	Dr Lee	you
city			
country			
job			
age			
flat/house			
married/single			
children			
languages			
other information			

5 Complete the table with information about you.

6 [Read Study Skill] Look at the paragraph about Dr Lee again. Underline the words *and* and *but* where they join sentences.

7 Join the sentences. Use *and* or *but*.

1 I am 18 years old. I am single.
2 I am from Turkey. I live in the capital, Ankara.
3 Joe comes from India. He is working in Germany at the moment.
4 Maria and Jose are married. They have four children.
5 Sam likes computers. He doesn't like computer games.
6 I want to build a big villa near my parents' house. I have no money.

8 Read the rules. Use the information from the table in exercise 4 to write a paragraph about you for a class journal. Start: **My name is …**

> **RULES** Present simple
>
> To describe people and what they do, use the Present Simple.
> When you write about yourself:
> *I live … In the evenings, I like …*
> When you write about other people:
> *George lives … He likes … They live … They like …*

Writing about people

9 Find out information about another student (or teacher). Make notes in your notebook. Write a paragraph about this person.

10 [Read Study Skill] Find nine mistakes in the sentences and correct them.

> My nam is Sonia I come from brazil. I am teacher in a school My husband work in bank. His name is riccardo. We have two childrens.

11 Read your two paragraphs and check your writing.

> **STUDY SKILL** Linking ideas (1)
>
> Use *and* or *but* to join sentences. Look at the examples:
> - *Hasan lives in Izmir. He works in an Internet café.*
>   *Hasan lives in Izmir* **and** *he works in an Internet café.*
> - *I understand Farsi. I don't speak it very well.*
>   *I understand Farsi,* **but** *I don't speak it very well.*
>
> Linking ideas makes your writing easier to follow.

> **STUDY SKILL** Checking your writing
>
> It is important to check that your writing is correct. Check:
> - spelling
> - capital letters
> - punctuation
> - grammar

VOCABULARY DEVELOPMENT Dictionary work (1)

1 **Read Study Skill** Match the parts of speech a–e in the Study Skill box with words 1–10 in the sentences.

> ## STUDY SKILL Parts of speech
>
> It is important to know the part of speech of a new word.
> Is it a/an … ?
>
> a **noun**: *a student*   d **adverb**: *always, quickly*
> b **verb**: *to study*   e **preposition**: *at, in, on*
> c **adjective**: *long*
>
> This knowledge will help you learn and use the word correctly.

`1 [ ]`   `2 [ ]`   `3 [ ]`   `4 [ ]`

1 Selina lives with her parents in the centre of town.

`5 [ ]`   `6 [ ]`   `7 [ ]`

2 We usually read textbooks or reports quite carefully.

`8 [ ]`   `9 [ ]`   `10 [ ]`

3 This is a very interesting novel, but the language is difficult.

2 **Read Study Skill** Look at the entries from the *Oxford Essential Dictionary*. Complete the table with information about the words.

> ## STUDY SKILL A dictionary entry (1)
>
> A dictionary gives you the meaning (or meanings) of a word.
> It also gives you other information, for example:
>
> - **pronunciation** (see phonetic symbols page 71)
> - **part of speech**
> - **example(s) of use**
>
> Get a good dictionary and learn how to use it!

suburb /'sʌbɜːb/ *noun*
one of the parts of a town or city outside the centre: *We live **in the suburbs**.*
▸ **suburban** /sə'bɜːbən/ *adjective*: *suburban areas*

quick 0─┳ /kwɪk/ *adjective, adverb*
(quicker, quickest)
taking little time ⊃ SAME MEANING **fast**: *It's quicker to travel by plane than by train.* ◇ *Can I make a quick telephone call?*
⊃ OPPOSITE **slow**
▸ **quickly** *adverb*: *Come as quickly as you can!*

check[1] 0─┳ /tʃek/ *verb* (checks, checking, checked /tʃekt/)
1 to look at something to see that it is right, good or safe: *Do the sums and then use a calculator to check your answers.* ◇ *Before driving off, I checked the oil and water.* ◇ *Check that all the windows are closed before you leave.*

always 0─┳ /'ɔːlweɪz/ *adverb*
1 at all times; every time: *I have always lived in London.* ◇ *The train is always late.*

word	pronunciation	part of speech	meaning	example
suburb	/'sʌbɜːb/	noun	one of the parts of a town or city outside the centre	We live in the suburbs.
quick				
check				
always				

3 **Read Study Skill** Organize the words in the box into three groups. Add more words to the table.

translator	sister	house	father	flat	builder	mother
apartment	accountant	cousin	villa	pilot	brother	
hostel	doctor	aunt	teacher	uncle	palace	professor

> ## STUDY SKILL Recording vocabulary (1)
>
> Your brain likes organization! When you learn new words, put them together in groups, for example jobs, family, homes.

jobs	family	homes

REVIEW

1 Use your dictionary to answer the questions.

  1 What part of speech is the word *how*?

  2 How many floors does a bungalow have?

  3 What is American English for the British noun *lorry*?

  4 What is the opposite of *difficult*?

  5 How do we pronounce *magazines*? Is it: /'maegəziːnz/, /mae'gəziːnz/, or /maegə'ziːnz/?

  6 What is the past tense of the verb *buy*?

  7 How do we spell the plural of *address*?

  8 What is the adjective of the noun *mathematics*?

  9 What is the name of a person who writes poetry?

 10 What is the missing word? We were late because our car broke _____ .

2 Look back at page 6. Study the rules about capital letters, full stops, and question marks again. Punctuate sentences 1–6.

  1 my friend igor comes from moscow

  2 i am studying french and history at manchester university

  3 is charles doing a course at capital institute

  4 my brother wants to visit turkey and germany next summer

  5 is there a message for mr hector ortiz from mexico

  6 the name of the hotel is al bustan palace it is just outside riyadh

3 Find words in Unit 1 to add to the groups. Add other words you know.

Things we read
novel, poem, …

Academic subjects
physics, English, …

4 Choose three words from Unit 1 that are new for you. Look them up in a dictionary. Complete the table.

word	pronunciation	part of speech	meaning	example

2 Daily routines

READING SKILLS Predicting content (1) • Skimming
WRITING SKILLS Handwriting • Paragraphs • Linking ideas (2) • Writing about routine and procedure
VOCABULARY DEVELOPMENT Collocations • Jobs ending in -er, -or, -ist

READING Work and stress

1 Work with a partner and complete the survey. How important are a–c when choosing a job? Write 1 = very important, 2 = quite important, or 3 = not important.

	me	my partner
a the job is healthy		
b the salary is good		
c the work is interesting		

Compare your answers with the class.

2 **Read Study Skill** Look at the people in the pictures on page 11. Answer the questions.

> ### STUDY SKILL Predicting content (1)
> Before you read, look at the pictures in a text. They can help you predict the content. They can tell you what the text is about and help you understand it.

1 What jobs do they do?   **A florist sells flowers.**
2 Are their jobs healthy or stressful?
   What do you think?

3 **Read Study Skill** Skim the article *Work and stress* to get the general idea. Choose a heading for each paragraph. There is one extra heading.

> ### STUDY SKILL Skimming
> Remember – **skimming** is reading very quickly to get the general idea from a text (a book, an article, a chapter, or just a paragraph).

☐ Eating healthy food   ☐ What people want
☐ Stressful jobs   ☐ Jobs that are healthy

4 Read the article. Were your predictions in exercise 2 correct?

5 Complete the summary of the article. Use the words in the box.

unhealthy   drives   interesting   salary   a florist   stress   traffic   healthy

> **Summary**
>
> Some jobs, for example ¹ _healthy_ , a personal trainer, and a nutritionist, are ² _____ . These jobs have very little ³ _____ or worry. Other jobs, however, are very ⁴ _____ . An example is a taxi driver. He ⁵ _____ people all day and often faces ⁶ _____ problems. It is difficult to get a job that is ⁷ _____ and healthy, and also has a good ⁸ _____ .

WORK AND STRESS

We all need to work in order to live. Some people are lucky with their work. This is because their jobs are healthy. What do we mean by 'healthy', and how can we find a 'healthy job'?

1 Jobs that are healthy.

Florists, personal trainers, professors, and nutritionists all have healthy jobs according to research. There are many reasons for this. A florist, for example, sells flowers and plants to customers. This is very relaxing work. A personal trainer, on the other hand, is usually very fit. He or she trains other people to lose weight and to keep fit. A nutritionist has a healthy job too. He or she knows all about healthy food and teaches people to eat well.

2 Stressful jobs.

However, research also shows that some jobs are 'unhealthy'. They cause a lot of stress and worry. For example, a taxi driver drives all day. He often faces traffic jams and difficult passengers too. A firefighter puts out dangerous fires and sometimes saves people from burning buildings. An MD (Managing Director) runs a large company. It is an interesting job, but it is also stressful. The MD has to keep everyone happy – the staff and the customers.

3

Most people are looking for the perfect job. They want a job that is interesting, with a good salary and not much stress. However, it is difficult to get everything. Healthy, relaxing jobs are usually not very well paid. On the other hand, people with stressful jobs often get good salaries. For example, the head of a big company gets a lot of money, but he or she does not always have good health, or the time to enjoy life.

BEFORE looking for a job, people should think carefully. What is most important for them? Is it money, health, or a job that is interesting? Then they can start their search. They may be lucky – and get everything they want!

WRITING Routines and procedures

1 [Read Study Skill] Look at the text about Matthias. It shows examples of six common mistakes in handwriting. Match a–f with examples 1–6.

a ☐ Letters are not clearly formed.
b ☐ Capital letters are not larger than small letters.
c ☐ There is not a space between each word.
d ☐ Letters do not point in the same direction.
e ☐ The letters are above the line or below.
f ☐ Lines do not start on the left hand side of the page.

STUDY SKILL Handwriting

Does everyone use a computer nowadays?
No! Sometimes you need to write by hand, for example:

- to make notes from a text/in a lecture
- for classwork/homework
- to draft an essay
- in exams
- for lists, postcards, or personal notes

Write clearly when you write by hand.

> **1** My name is Matthias. I am 22 years
> **2** old and I am astudent at auniversity
> in Berlin in Germany. I am studying
> chemical engineering. I live in a
> student hostel on the university **3**
> campus. I am going to finish my course
> **4** next semester, so I am working
> hard to pass my exams. When I **5**
> leave the university, I want to go
> **6** overseas to continue my studies. I would
> like to do a Master's degree. One day I
> would like to work for an oil company.

2 [Read Study Skill] Look at the text about Helena. What is wrong with the organization?

> My sister, Helena, is an English teacher. She teaches in a secondary school in Lisbon, Portugal. The school is near her flat, so she usually walks to work.
>
> She arrives at work at 8 o'clock in the morning and she leaves school at about 3 or 4 in the afternoon. In the evenings she marks homework and prepares lessons for the following day.
>
> At the weekends she is also busy, but with her family and friends. She shops for food at the local market, visits relatives, and spends time with her husband.
>
> In summer, if the weather is good, she likes having a barbecue with friends and family by the beach.

STUDY SKILL Paragraphs

Write in **paragraphs**. There are two styles for paragraphs:

- block   ■ indented

A paragraph usually contains at least three sentences. Do not start each sentence on a new line. Do not write one-sentence paragraphs.

3 Write the text again on lined paper as two paragraphs. Use the block or the indented style. Write clearly.

4 **Read Study Skill** Read the sentences about Maria's daily routine at university. Circle the sequencing words.

Paragraph 1

- ⬜ (Then) she goes to her first class. This is at 9 o'clock.
- ⬜ First, she has a cup of tea in the snack bar.
- ⬜ After that, she goes to the library and studies for an hour before lunch.
- ☑ 1 Maria usually gets to the university at about 8.30.
- ⬜ At 11 o'clock she has another class. This is poetry.

Paragraph 2

- ⬜ They talk about their studies or their plans for the weekend.
- ⬜ Finally, she leaves the university at about 5. It is a long day.
- ⬜ After the class she goes to the library again for another hour.
- ☑ 6 At about 1 o'clock Maria goes to the student canteen with some of her friends.
- ⬜ In the afternoon Maria has one more class from 2 o'clock to 3.30.

5 Use the sequencing words and time expressions to help you put sentences 1–10 in order.

6 Read about the procedure Maria follows to write an essay. Complete the paragraph with words from the box.

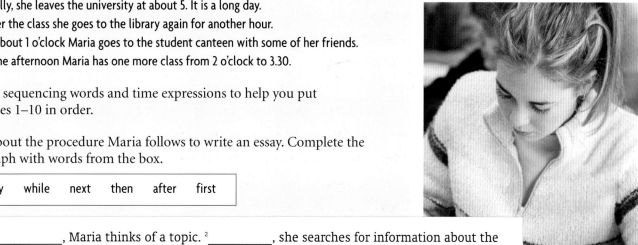

> finally   while   next   then   after   first

¹_____, Maria thinks of a topic. ²_____, she searches for information about the topic and reads all she can. She makes notes about the subject ³_____ she is reading. ⁴_____ that, she uses her notes to write a plan for the essay. ⁵_____ she is ready to write the essay. She usually writes on the computer. She rewrites parts of the essay again and again until she is happy with it. ⁶_____, she checks the essay very carefully for punctuation, grammar, and spelling before giving it to her lecturer.

Writing about routine and procedure

7 Interview your partner. What is his/her daily routine at school/college/university? Write two paragraphs. Use ideas from the box .

> gets to / leaves (the university/school) ...   First, then, next, after that, ...
> has (tea/coffee/lunch) ...   At (...) o'clock ...
> goes to (the first class / the library) ...   In the morning / In the afternoon ...
> studies ...   After / before ...

8 How do you revise for an important exam? Write a paragraph to describe the procedure you follow. Use ideas from the box.

Start: **To revise for an important exam, first I ...**

> make a study plan   look at the syllabus   find a quiet place to
> study   make notes   take breaks   remember the main points

STUDY SKILL Linking ideas (2)

To describe a daily routine (working, studying, etc.) or a procedure (writing an essay, applying for a job), use:

- **sequencing words** to say one thing happens after another, for example: *first, after, then, finally.*
- **time expressions** to say when, for example: *at 1 o'clock, in the evening.*

Note If two things happen at the same time, use *while*. For example: *I listen to the radio **while** I am having breakfast.*

VOCABULARY DEVELOPMENT Words that go together

1 [Read Study Skill] Match the verbs 1–7 with words or phrases a–g.

1 [e] put out   a   research
2 [ ] fill in   b   fit
3 [ ] run   c   telephone calls
4 [ ] make   d   a company
5 [ ] send   e   fires
6 [ ] do   f   a form
7 [ ] keep   g   emails

2 Complete the sentences with the correct verb. Use a dictionary to help you find the collocation of the underlined word.

1 At the weekend Sami _____ <u>a walk</u> in the park.
2 Last week Hasan _____ <u>an accident</u> in his new pick-up truck.
3 Can you _____ me <u>the time</u> of the next flight to Bangkok?
4 Igor usually _____ <u>the 11.30 train</u> to Moscow from St Petersburg.
5 Exercise helps people to _____ <u>weight</u>.
6 Shall we _____ <u>a taxi</u> to the airport?

3 How many collocations can you think of for *computer* and *business*? Use your dictionary to help. Draw diagrams.

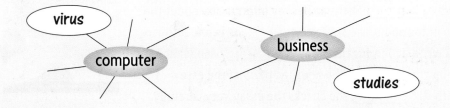

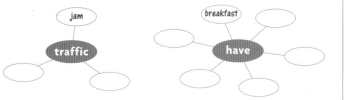
Spelling (1)

4 Read the rules. Complete the definitions.

1 A s_____ does research in science.
2 A d_____ helps sick people.
3 A sh_____ sells things.
4 A f_____ sells flowers.
5 An a_____ acts in plays and films.
6 An i_____ interprets from one language to another.

RULES Jobs ending in *-er*, *-or*, *-ist*

Many jobs end in *-er* and *-or*. Others end in *-ist*.

For example: *taxi driver*; *professor*; *journalist*

5 Write the jobs in exercise 4 in the table. Add other jobs.

-er	-or	-ist
taxi driver	professor	journalist

REVIEW

1 Choose five jobs from Unit 2. Write a sentence about each. Describe what the people do. For example,

a taxi driver   A taxi driver drives people from one place to another.

a florist   A florist sells flowers and plants to customers.

2 Complete the paragraph about Sam's day with the sentences in the box.

> Then he goes to his office.
> First he has a quick breakfast in the hotel coffee shop.
> Finally, at about 4 o'clock Sam leaves work.
> After that, he has a meeting with his manager.
> In the afternoon, he goes back to his office.
> Next, he speaks to the hotel staff.

Sam is the assistant manager of a big hotel in Hong Kong. It is a busy hotel and his day starts very early. He gets to work at about 7 o'clock. [1]_____ He usually just has tea and toast. [2]_____ He starts up his computer and checks his emails. There are always a lot of messages. [3]_____ He asks them about any problems in the kitchens, or with the guests. [4]_____ They find solutions to problems, and discuss improvements and other changes to the hotel. At about 1 o'clock he has lunch. [5]_____ He sends a few more emails and makes some telephone calls. [6]_____ On his way home he collects his children from school, and arrives home at about 5.30.

3 How do you get information on a topic from the Internet? Write down the steps. Check your list with another student. Then write a paragraph to describe the procedure.

Start: **To get information from the Internet, first I ...**

4 Find nouns that go with the verbs in table A, and verbs that go with the nouns in table B. Use a dictionary to help.

A

verb	noun
save	time, money
face	
train	
scan	
spend	

B

verb	noun
have, go for	lunch
	emails
	telephone calls
	a meeting
	the computer

3 People and the environment

READING SKILLS Scanning – using headings • Meaning from context
WRITING SKILLS Punctuation (2) • Talking about frequency • Writing about study habits
RESEARCH Sources
VOCABULARY DEVELOPMENT   Recording vocabulary (2)

READING Weather

1 Look at the pictures of weather. Match the titles 1–3 with the pictures a–c.

1 ☐ Desert morning
2 ☐ A winter's day
3 ☐ Hurricane season

2 Match the words with the pictures in exercise 1.

a heavy rain	☐ snow	☐ sunny	☐ cold
☐ dry	☐ blue sky	☐ wet	☐ warm
☐ strong winds	☐ hot	☐ storm	☐ ice

3 Work with a partner. Use the words to talk about the pictures. What countries do you think they are in?

4 With your partner, discuss answers to the questions. Make a note of your ideas.

1 Do hurricanes have names?
2 What's the difference between a hurricane and a typhoon?
3 How do we measure hurricanes?
4 What is the centre of a hurricane called?
5 In what seasons are there hurricanes?

5 **Read Study Skill** Scan the encyclopaedia entry *Hurricanes* to check your answers to exercise 4. Use the headings to help. Were your ideas right?

STUDY SKILL Scanning – using headings

Scanning is reading quickly to find information.

One way to scan for information is to use the headings of paragraphs, sections, and chapters. For example, to find the answer to question 1 in exercise 4, *Do hurricanes have names?* look in the encyclopaedia entry under the heading *Naming hurricanes*.

HURRICANES

What are hurricanes?

Hurricanes are very big storms. They usually form in the warm waters of the Atlantic Ocean, the Caribbean Sea, and the Gulf of Mexico. Hurricanes also form in other parts of the world, but they have different names. In the Pacific Ocean, near Japan, China, and the Philippines, they are called 'typhoons'.

How do they form?

Hurricanes rotate anti-clockwise around an 'eye'. This is the centre of the storm. They move across the warm oceans and grow bigger and stronger. They cause heavy rain, strong winds, and <u>huge</u> waves at sea. Most hurricanes stay at sea, but <u>occasionally</u> they come onto the land. Then they cause a lot of damage to buildings, trees, and cars.

Measuring hurricanes

We measure hurricanes by categories – from 1 to 5. A Category 1 hurricane is the weakest. It has winds of between 119 and 153 kms per hour. A Category 5 hurricane is the strongest. The winds are more than 249 kms per hour. This is a very dangerous hurricane. Fortunately, there are not many Category 5 hurricanes.

Naming hurricanes

All hurricanes have names. In this way, we can <u>track</u> the storms as they move across the ocean. Hurricanes always have men's or women's names. The first storm of the season begins with the letter A, for example Andrew. The second begins with the letter B, for example Bertha, and so on.

Hurricane seasons

In the Atlantic the hurricane season is in the summer and autumn. It starts on 1 June and <u>continues</u> until 30 November. Occasionally, there are hurricanes at other times of the year. The <u>peak</u> is in September. This is when the sea is very warm. This <u>region</u> has about six hurricanes a year. However, in the north-west Pacific there are hurricanes (typhoons) all the year round.

6 **Read Study Skill** Read the encyclopaedia extract again carefully. Guess the meaning of the underlined words. First identify the parts of speech (*noun, verb, adjective, adverb*). Then choose meanings from the box to complete the table.

the high point   goes on   sometimes   part of the world   follow   very big

	part of speech	meaning
1 huge		
2 occasionally		
3 track		
4 continues		
5 peak		
6 region		

STUDY SKILL Meaning from context

Sometimes you can guess the meaning of a word from the words around it, that is, the **context**. Identifying the part of speech also helps. Look at the example, *rotate*:

Hurricanes <u>rotate</u> **anti-clockwise around** an 'eye'.

The word *Hurricanes* helps you identify the part of speech.

1 What part of speech is <u>rotate</u>:
   a noun, a verb, an adjective, an adverb?

The words **anti-clockwise**, **around**, help you guess the meaning.

2 What does <u>rotate</u> mean:
   get bigger, move in a circle, rain a lot?

WRITING Describing our lives

1 **Read Study Skill** Look at sentences 1–4. Which *'s* endings show possession? Which are contractions?

1 Nori's got a puncture.
2 Nori's car is in the garage.
3 Nori's late.
4 Have you got Nori's phone number?

2 Put apostrophes in the sentences where necessary.

1 Have you got the girls books? Shes looking for them.
2 My favourite seasons are spring and summer.
   The weathers beautiful then.
3 The students exam results were very bad. They all have
   to retake them.
4 Dont swim today. The waves are huge and theyre very dangerous!
5 In the winter months many students go skiing in the mountains.
6 **A** Wheres Mikes computer?   **B** Ive got it here.

STUDY SKILL Punctuation (2)

Use **apostrophes** for:

■ **possession** (belonging to someone/something). For example:
  the **boy's** computer = **his** computer (singular)
  the **boys'** computer = **their** computer (plural)
■ **contractions** (missing letters). For example:
  I'm (I am), doesn't (does not), the student's (the student has/is)

In formal writing do not use contractions, but you can use an apostrophe for possession.

Find two words with apostrophes in the article *Hurricanes*.

3 Read the essay on deserts. Underline seven contractions. Write the full form.

Deserts

They are

Deserts cover about one-fifth of the Earth's area. They're defined as regions where the rainfall's less than 250mm (or 10 inches) a year. In some years there's no rainfall at all. Deserts don't have much vegetation because of their dry climate. They're usually covered by sand or stones. As a result, most animals can't live there, except for a few, such as camels, foxes, and some insects. There are hot and cold deserts. The world's largest hot desert is the Sahara. There are other hot deserts in Australia, southern Africa, and the Middle East. They have a very high temperature in the summer, over 40°C. The icy continent of Antarctica is an example of a cold desert. It doesn't rain, but it occasionally snows.

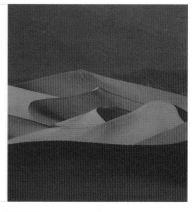

4 Read the paragraph describing how Julia spends her summer. Circle the adverbs of frequency. What do you notice about the adverb *sometimes*? Read and complete the rules.

RULES Talking about frequency

When you describe a routine, use adverbs of frequency to say how often you do something. For example:
*Hadi **usually** drives to the college.*
*Beth is **sometimes** late with her essays.*

Complete the rules. Write *before* or *after*.
a With the verb *to be*, the adverb of frequency comes _____ the main verb.
b With other verbs, the adverb of frequency comes _____ the main verb.

Complete the list of adverbs from 100% of the time to 0% of the time.
(100%) ◄─────────────────────────────► (0%)
always _____ often _____ _____

Julia's summer

In the summer we always go to our dacha in the countryside, just outside Moscow. A dacha is a kind of wooden summer house. We have a small garden with some fruit trees, and we grow vegetables too. We eat our meals in the garden. The weather is usually warm and sunny at that time of the year, but it sometimes rains. There is a lake near our dacha. My brothers like swimming and they often go there. The water is always freezing cold, so I never swim. I prefer to stay in the garden and read. Sometimes the whole family goes for a walk in the forest and we collect mushrooms for the evening meal. I do not usually cook, but I love making mushroom soup. We really enjoy our summers in the dacha.

5 Write a paragraph about your summer. Use ideas from the box and adverbs of freqency.

> play sports   stay at home   visit friends/family   go camping
> go to the beach/mountains/park   go swimming   have picnics

6 Look at the *Study habits questionnaire*. Write the words in the correct order to make questions 1–6.

Study habits questionnaire

1 _____? do / where / you / study / to / like

  a at home   **b** in a library   **c** other place

2 _____? usually / study / when / you / do

  a in the morning   **b** in the afternoon   **c** in the evening   **d** at night

3 _____? to / study / do / how / prefer / you

  a alone   **b** with a friend   **c** in a study group

4 _____? make / you / notes / do / when you study

  a always   **b** usually   **c** sometimes   **d** never

5 _____? study / many / do / how / you / hours / in a week

  a 0–2 hours   **b** 3–6   **c** 7–10   **d** more than 10

6 _____? make / do / study-plan / how often / you / a

  a never   **b** every day   **c** every week

---

7 Read about Suresh's study habits. Circle his answers on the questionnaire above.

> I am a student at Global Institute. After my classes at the Institute I like to study in the library. I usually go there in the afternoon for one or two hours. Sometimes I study at home, but not often because it is very noisy. I prefer to study alone. Sometimes friends ask me to study with them, but we usually start chatting about other things. I always make notes when I study. It helps me to remember. In a week I think I study about eight hours. Of course, I also have 16 hours of lectures. At the beginning of every week I make a study plan for the whole week. I am always busy!

8 Answer the questionnaire about yourself. Make notes in your notebook giving reasons for your answers.

9 Use the questionnaire to interview another student. Ask *Why …?* to find out reasons for his/her answers. Make notes. What study habits do you share?

10 ┃ Read Study Skill ┃ Make a study plan for yourself. Decide what to study and when. For example:

	a.m.	p.m.
Monday	9–11 Management	2–6 Accounting
Tuesday	8–10 Statistics	7–9 English

Writing about study habits

11 Write a paragraph about your study habits. Use your answers from the questionnaire to help.

STUDY SKILL How to be a good student

Everyone has his or her own way of studying, but here are a few tips:
- Find a quiet place to study.
- Study when you are fresh, not tired.
- Get plenty of exercise and sleep.
- Find a study partner or partners – it can help.
- Take notes when you read.
- Make a study plan for the week.

RESEARCH Finding information (1)

1 **Read Study Skill** Complete the diagram with possible sources of information. Share your ideas with the class.

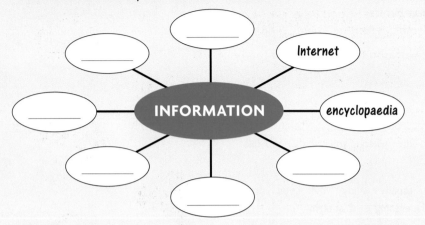

STUDY SKILL Sources

If you need information on a topic (hurricanes, deserts, etc.), you need a reliable **source**. There are many different sources of information, for example the Internet and encyclopaedias.

Remember – it is important to make a careful note of the sources you refer to (website, date, encyclopaedia title, publisher).

2 Decide what sources you will use to find the answers to 1–9. Try to use a different source for each one.

		source	answer
1	a definition of the word *search*	dictionary	look for something
2	the temperature today in Singapore	observation	
3	the date when Tutenkhamun died		
4	the names of the countries which border Bhutan		
5	the time of sunset today in your country		
6	What is the *law of gravity*?		
7	the origin of the food 'pasta'		
8	the birthplace of Mahatma Ghandi		
9	the most popular make of mobile phone among students in your class		

3 Find the answers to 1–9 in exercise 2. First decide which words to use in your searches. Compare answers with a partner.

VOCABULARY DEVELOPMENT Drawing and diagrams

Read Study Skill Look up the words *building*, *clockwise*, *track* in a dictionary. Draw pictures to help you remember them.

STUDY SKILL Recording vocabulary (2)

Your brain likes pictures! Use drawings and diagrams to help you remember words. For example:

wind   wave   damage   rotate

You can also visualize a picture to go with the word.

peak

Or you can draw a diagram to grade a group of words. For example:

↑ huge	↑ country
very big	city
big	town
small	village

REVIEW

1 Complete the table with words about the weather. Use your dictionary to find the right part of speech.

noun	adjective	verb
snow		to snow
	windy	
		to ice over
rain		
	cloudy	to cloud over
sun		
	warm	
heat		
fog		

2 Choose five words from Unit 3. Draw visuals to help you remember the words. Compare with a partner.

3 Put the words in the right order to make sentences.
1 months / form / usually / in / summer / the / hurricanes
2 weekend / never / at / studies / Tony / the
3 are / night / at / cold / sometimes / deserts
4 to / don't / very / cinema / often / I / go / the
5 India / September / in / beautiful / always / weather / in / the / is

4 Rewrite the sentences with the adverb of frequency.
1 Maureen likes studying at night. (usually)
2 Why is Yuki late for work? (always)
3 It rains in the summer where I live. (never)
4 I read the newspaper. (often)
5 The winters are long and cold in my country. (usually)
6 Kim stays at home at weekends. (sometimes)

5 Complete the sentences using the verbs *read, interview, look up, surf, consult.*
1 I often _____ new words in a dictionary.
2 If you _____ the Internet, you can find a lot of useful information.
3 The student was not sure when Tutenkhamun died, so he had to _____ an encyclopaedia.
4 The researcher will _____ several students to find out about their study habits.
5 Maria has to _____ three science textbooks by the end of the week.

4 Architecture

READING Famous buildings

1 Work with a partner. Look at the photos of the Taj Mahal and the Bank of China Tower. Discuss the questions. Use words from the box to help.

old	modern	tall	style	marble	steel
glass	stone	city	gardens	architect	

1 How are the two buildings different?
2 What do you think they are made of?
3 Where are they situated?
4 Who do you think built them? Why?

Taj Mahal

Bank of China Tower

2 **Read Study Skill** Read the texts about the two buildings. Make notes to complete the table.

STUDY SKILL Making notes (1)

Making notes is an important skill. Use it for study or intensive reading. Read slowly and carefully when you make notes. Note-making helps you:

- **understand** what you read
- **remember** the important points
- **write** about the topic.
- **revise** later for exams

There are many ways of making notes. Drawing and labelling diagrams is a kind of note-making.

building	Taj Mahal	
built by		
located	Agra, north of India	
date		
building type		skyscraper
made of		glass, steel
style	Islamic	
other information	Some say – most beautiful building in the world	

3 Read the texts again. Label the diagrams of the two buildings.

4 Look at the underlined words from the two texts. What part of speech are they: *noun, verb,* or *adjective*? Guess the meanings from the context. The words in bold will help.

1 It was a <u>tomb</u> for his **wife**, Mumtaz Mahal, who **died** in 1631.
2 It is **built** in an Islamic **style**. It <u>symbolizes</u> Shah Jehan's **love** for his wife.
3 The **architect** was Ieoh Ming Pei. He is very well known. He <u>designs</u> large, unusual **buildings**.
4 It is a **very tall** <u>skyscraper</u> with 70 floors. It is **367 metres** high.
5 There is a small viewing platform, which is open to the public. The platform is on the **42nd floor**, so **visitors** can have a <u>panoramic</u> **view of the whole city**.

The **Taj Mahal** is located in Agra, in the north of India. Many people think it is the most beautiful building in the world. It is situated in formal gardens just outside the city, so it is in a very quiet place. Nearby there is a river. The Taj Mahal was built between 1631 and 1654 by Shah Jehan. It was a tomb for his wife, Mumtaz Mahal, who died in 1631. It is built in an Islamic style. It symbolizes Shah Jehan's love for his wife. In the centre of the building is the tomb, which is made of white marble. The rest of the building is made of sandstone. Around the tomb there are four tall minarets.

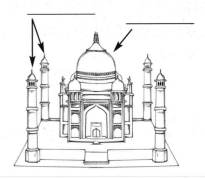

The **Bank of China Tower** is situated in Hong Kong. The architect was Ieoh Ming Pei. He is very well known. He designs large, unusual buildings. The Bank of China Tower was built between 1982 and 1990. It is a very tall skyscraper with 70 floors. It is 367 metres high. The style of the building is modern and it symbolizes strength and growth. The building is very light inside because it is made of glass and steel. There is a small viewing platform, which is open to the public. The platform is on the 42nd floor, so visitors can have a panoramic view of the whole city. It is one of the tallest buildings in Hong Kong and is used for offices.

height = _____ m.

floors = _____

5 Use your notes to complete the summary about the Taj Mahal.

Summary

The Taj Mahal was built by ¹_____ between the years ²_____ and ³_____.
It is located in ⁴_____ , in the north of India. It is a ⁵_____ for Jehan's wife. It is made of
⁶_____ and ⁷_____. The style is ⁸_____.

6 Write a summary of the text about the Bank of China Tower. Use your notes from exercise 2.

RESEARCH Finding information (2)

Read Study Skill Choose a famous building from the box, or from your country. Find information about it and make notes in the table.

Jin Mao Building – Shanghai	Empire State Building – New York
Tokyo City Hall	Sydney Opera House	Blue Mosque – Istanbul
Petronas Towers – Kuala Lumpur	Burj Al Arab – Dubai

STUDY SKILL Focusing your search

Before you search for information about a topic, for example a building, ask yourself: *What do I need to know?*

Make a list of things you want to find out. For example: *Who was it built by? Where is it located?*

building	
built by	
other information	

WRITING   Describing buildings

1 **Read Study Skill** Find a sentence with *because* in the paragraph about the Bank of China Tower.

2 Complete the sentences with a reason clause.

   1 A lot of people visit the Taj Mahal because …

   2 Some people do not like skyscrapers because …

   3 Some jobs are unhealthy because …

   4 Most plants cannot grow in deserts because …

   5 I like _____ (name of a building) because …

3 **Read Study Skill** Find sentences with *so* in the texts about the Taj Mahal and the Bank of China Tower. Underline *so* and circle the commas.

> **STUDY SKILL** Linking ideas (3)
>
> **Reason clauses – *because***
>
> Use *because* to join sentences. It tells you the **reason** (why/why not?) something happens. Look at sentences **a** and **b**. Underline *because*.
>
> **a** *The building gets very hot in summer. It is made of glass.*
>
> **b** *The building gets very hot in summer because it is made of glass.*

> **STUDY SKILL** Linking ideas (4)
>
> **Result clauses – *so***
>
> Use *so* to join sentences. It tells you the **result** of something. Look at sentences **a** and **b**. Underline *so*, and circle the comma.
>
> **a** *The building is made of glass. It gets very hot in summer.*
>
> **b** *The building is made of glass, so it gets very hot in summer.*

4 Match sentences 1–5 with a–e. Rewrite them as one sentence using *so*. Don't forget the comma.

1 ☐ Sometimes we just want to get information.	a He is learning everything about software.
2 ☐ A personal diary is only for ourselves.	b We read the text quickly to find it.
3 ☐ George wants to work for a computer company one day.	c This is when hurricanes usually form.
4 ☐ Taxi drivers face traffic jams every day.	d They often suffer from stress in their work.
5 ☐ In the summer the oceans are very warm.	e We write in a very informal way.

5 Complete the sentences with a result clause.

   1 There is a viewing platform on the 42nd floor, so …
   you can have a view of the city.

   2 The Taj Mahal is a very beautiful building, so …

   3 There is a lift to the top of the tower, so …

   4 Deserts are very dry regions, so …

   5 Marble is a very expensive material, so …

   6 It is very hot in Mexico in the summer, so …

6 Match sentences 1–5 with a–f. Rewrite them as one sentence using *because* or *so*. Use a comma where necessary.

1 ☐ I want to visit the Louvre in Paris.	a Most of the buildings are tall and narrow.
2 ☐ Paulo likes climbing mountains.	b He is going to Switzerland for his holidays.
3 ☐ Nora wants to work for a newspaper as a journalist.	c She loves writing and enjoys meeting people.
4 ☐ Land is very expensive in Hong Kong.	d They want to get away from the noisy cities and stay in a quiet place.
5 ☐ India has a lot of rain in the summer months.	e It is better to visit the country in the dry season.
6 ☐ In Russia people like to go to their 'dachas' in the summer.	f It has some beautiful paintings.

7 Complete the description *The Tower Houses of Yemen*. Use the words and phrases in the box.

> because   so   are made of   there is   there are   have   were built
> on the outside   in the centre   are located

The Tower Houses of Yemen

The Tower Houses of Yemen ¹_____ in the old city of Sana'a, the capital of Yemen. These houses are very beautiful and unusual, ²_____ many visitors come to Yemen to see them. They ³_____ by local builders and they are hundreds of years old. They ⁴_____ stone and brick. The buildings are tall and they ⁵_____ at least five floors. ⁶_____ of the house is the main staircase. This goes up to all of the floors. The family members usually live on the upper floors. They do not live on the ground floor or the first floor ⁷_____ these floors are for food and animals. On the top floor ⁸_____ usually a large sitting room. Visitors come there to chat and drink tea. ⁹_____ walls of the buildings there are beautiful decorations, such as stars and snakes. ¹⁰_____ also decorations around the windows and the doors.

8 ▐ Read Study Skill ▐ Find examples of descriptive words and phrases in *The Tower Houses of Yemen*. Underline them.

<u>The Tower Houses of Yemen are located ...</u>

9 Find a result clause and a reason clause in the description of *The Tower Houses of Yemen*. Write out the result and reason clauses.

Writing about a building

10 Look again at the notes you made about a famous building on page 23. Write a description of the building.

VOCABULARY DEVELOPMENT Dictionary work (2)

1 | Read Study Skill | Find the adjective *light* in the text about the *Bank of China Tower* on page 23. In this context, what does *light* mean?

STUDY SKILL A dictionary entry (2)

Many words in English have more than one meaning. Make sure you use the correct meaning. For example:

The adjective *light* has four meanings. Look at the dictionary entry.

light² 0━ /laɪt/ *adjective* (lighter, lightest)
1 full of natural light: *In summer it's light until about ten o'clock.* ◊ *The room has a lot of windows so it's very light.* ⟳ OPPOSITE **dark**
2 with a pale colour: *a light blue shirt* ⟳ OPPOSITE **dark**
3 easy to lift or move: *Will you carry this bag for me? It's very light.* ⟳ OPPOSITE **heavy** ⟳ Look at the picture at **heavy**.
4 not very much or not very strong: *light rain* ◊ *I had a light breakfast.*
▶ **lightly** /'laɪtli/ *adverb*: *She touched me lightly on the arm.*

---

2 Look at the dictionary entries. They show definitions for the adjectives *poor*, *rich*, *hard*, and *cool*. How many meanings are there for each adjective?

3 Match the underlined adjectives in the sentences to the meanings in the dictionary entries. Write the number. For example:

Pierre's exam results were very poor. He has to take the exams again. ___3___
People who come from poor families usually work hard. ___1___

1 a I feel sick. Sonia's cake was too <u>rich</u> for me. _____
   b Bill Gates is a <u>rich</u> man and he gives a lot of money to charity. _____
   c Rome is a very old city. It is <u>rich</u> in history. _____

2 a Diamond is a <u>hard</u> material. It is used in industry for cutting. _____
   b It is very <u>hard</u> to learn a new language. It takes time. _____

3 a The pilot was very <u>cool</u> when the engine caught fire. _____
   b Hong Kong is great fun. It's a really <u>cool</u> city. _____
   c Summers in Sweden are <u>cool</u>, but usually quite sunny. _____

4 Find the nouns *rest* and *view* in the texts about the Taj Mahal and the Bank of China Tower on page 23. Use the dictionary entries to check the meanings.

5 | Read Study Skill | Look at the nouns in the box. Are they countable (**C**) or uncountable (**U**)? Check in your dictionary.

STUDY SKILL Countable or uncountable nouns?

Your dictionary tells you if a noun is countable, that is, if it has a plural form. For example: **building** (*buildings*), **architect** (*architects*).
There are five new **buildings** *in our street.* (countable)

Uncountable nouns have no plural form, for example: **time**, **oil**.
We haven't got much **time** *– let's go!* (uncountable)

| book **C**   time **U**   information ___   floor ___   public ___ |
| platform ___   steel ___   rain ___   tomb ___   garden ___ |

---

6 What is different about the nouns *glass* and *marble*? Check in your dictionary.

---

poor 0━ /pɔː(r)/ *adjective* (poorer, poorest)
1 with very little money: *She was too poor to buy clothes for her children.* ◊ *She gave her life to helping* **the poor** (= poor people). ⟳ The noun is **poverty**. ⟳ OPPOSITE **rich**
3 bad: *My grandfather is in very poor health.*

rich 0━ /rɪtʃ/ *adjective* (richer, richest)
1 having a lot of money: *a rich family* ◊ *It's a favourite resort for* **the rich** (= people who are rich) *and famous.* ⟳ OPPOSITE **poor**
2 containing a lot of something: *Oranges are rich in vitamin C.*
3 Food that is **rich** has a lot of fat or sugar in it and makes you feel full quickly: *a rich chocolate cake*

hard¹ 0━ /hɑːd/ *adjective* (harder, hardest)
1 not soft: *These apples are very hard.* ◊ *I couldn't sleep because the bed was too hard.* ⟳ OPPOSITE **soft**
2 difficult to do or understand: *The exam was very hard.* ◊ *hard work* ⟳ OPPOSITE **easy**

cool¹ 0━ /kuːl/ *adjective* (cooler, coolest)
1 a little cold; not hot or warm: *cool weather* ◊ *I'd like a cool drink.* ⟳ Look at the note at **cold**.
2 not excited or angry ⟳ SAME MEANING **calm**
3 (*informal*) very good or fashionable: *Those are cool shoes you're wearing!*

rest¹ 0━ /rest/ *noun*
1 **the rest** the part that is left or the ones that are left: *If you don't want the rest, I'll eat it.* ◊ *I liked the beginning, but* **the rest** *of the film wasn't very good.* ◊ *Jason watched TV and the rest of us went for a walk.*
2 a time when you relax, sleep or do nothing: *After walking for an hour, we stopped for a rest.*

view 0━ /vjuː/ *noun*
1 what you believe or think about something ⟳ SAME MEANING **opinion**: *He has* **strong views** *on marriage.* ◊ *In my view, she has done nothing wrong.*
2 what you can see from a place: *There were beautiful* **views** *of the mountains all around.* ◊ *At the top of the hill, the lake* **came into view** (= could be seen).

REVIEW

1 Complete the diagram with types of building material using words from Unit 4. Add other words.

2 Label the diagram of a house. Use the words in the box and your dictionary to help.

- [ ] roof
- [ ] walls
- [ ] stairs
- [ ] door
- [ ] window
- [ ] garden
- [ ] ground floor
- [ ] first floor
- [ ] second floor
- [ ] kitchen
- [ ] bathroom
- [ ] garage
- [ ] bedroom
- [ ] living room
- [ ] gate
- [ ] terrace

3 Complete the description of the house in the diagram in exercise 2. Use the words and phrases in the box.

> in the centre   around   there is   on the left   has   is made
> of   on the right   there are   was built   is located

The house ¹_____ in the suburbs, not far from the city centre. It ²_____ in 2006 and ³_____ stone and concrete. The style is modern and very simple. It ⁴_____ a flat roof and three floors. The garden is quite large and well designed. ⁵_____ of the house is a garage and ⁶_____ there is a terrace with plants. ⁷_____ several palm trees around the house and ⁸_____ of the garden is a small pond. The house has four bedrooms and three bathrooms. There are high walls ⁹_____ the garden and ¹⁰_____ a steel gate at the front.

4 Result or reason? Rewrite sentences **a** and **b** as one sentence, using *because* or *so*.

1 **a** Glass is a cheap and light material.
   b It is used in many modern buildings.

2 **a** Everyone wants to visit the Burj Al Arab.
   b It is a very famous and unusual building.

3 **a** It is important to take good notes.
   b They help you to understand what you read.

4 **a** Shah Jehan decided to build a beautiful tomb for his wife.
   b He loved her very much.

5 **a** Winters in Russia are very cold.
   b It is important to wear warm clothes.

6 **a** The weather was perfect.
   b They decided to have lunch in the garden.

5 Education

READING Universities

1 Work with a partner. Look at the pictures and answer the questions.

1 Match pictures a–c with the universities.

☐ Harvard University, USA

☐ Oxford University, UK

☐ Moscow State University, Russia

2 What famous universities do you know?

3 What is a good age to be a university student? Can you be too old or too young? Why/Why not?

2 [Read Study Skill] Skim the title and the first paragraph of the newspaper article *Too Young for Oxford?* Answer the questions.

1 What is the article about?

2 What information from a–d will it give?

a ☐ a history of the city of Oxford

b ☐ information about Oxford University

c ☐ different types of schools in Britain

d ☐ what is special about the young boy

3 Which five words from the box will you find in the article?

| swim   wedding   family   concert   intelligent |
| passport   examinations   school   knife   teachers |

> **STUDY SKILL** Predicting content (2)
>
> Before you read the whole text, read the title and the first few sentences.
> Make predictions about the content of the text.
> - the topic   (What is it about?)
> - information (What information will it give?)
> - vocabulary   (What words will you find?)
>
> Predicting will help you read. It will also tell you if a text is useful before you read it.

3 Read the article quickly to check your predictions in exercise 2.

4 Complete definitions 1–6 with the underlined words in the article.

1 _____ *adjective*: like an adult, fully grown

2 _____ *noun*: a very clever person

3 _____ *verb*: to say or think the opposite

4 _____ *noun*: a big organization like a bank, hospital, prison, or school

5 _____ *adjective*: able to speak or write a language easily and correctly

6 _____ *verb*: to go to or to be present at

Too young for Oxford?

Yinan Wang is a 14-year-old Chinese boy. In a few months he will be a student at Oxford University, in the United Kingdom, one of the most famous academic <u>institutions</u> in the world. Many people are asking, 'Isn't he too young to <u>attend</u> a university?'

Two years ago, Yinan Wang was a student at a school in Beijing, in China. Then his father got a job at an aerospace company near London, so the whole family moved from Beijing to London. Yinan Wang continued his studies at a very large secondary school near their home.

When he arrived in England, Yinan Wang could only speak a few words of English. 'At first I was very lonely', he says. 'I couldn't speak to anyone, so I couldn't make friends.' However, his teachers could see that he was very intelligent. In fact, he was a <u>genius</u>. He was especially good at mathematics and science.

Now, two years later, Yinan Wang is going to Oxford University to study science. At the age of 14, he is one of the youngest students to study at this famous university. However, his schoolteachers think he will have no problems. One teacher says, 'He had special classes in English and he is now <u>fluent</u>. He also recently got 98% in a university maths exam.'

Yinan Wang is not the first child to go to Oxford University. Ruth Lawrence was only 13 when she went to Oxford to study mathematics. However, are young teenagers really <u>mature</u> enough for university? Many universities do not take students below the age of 17 or 18. People say they cannot enjoy university life. Other people <u>disagree</u> and say that very clever children should not wait.

5 Read the article slowly and carefully. Choose a, b, or c to complete sentences 1–3.

> 1 Yinan's family moved to London because ...
>   a he got a place at Oxford University.
>   b he wanted to learn English.
>   c his father got a job near London.
>
> 2 When Yinan came to England, he ...
>   a had a lot of friends.
>   b could not make any friends.
>   c did not want any English friends.
>
> 3 Yinan's teachers think that he will ...
>   a have problems at Oxford University.
>   b need special classes in English.
>   c not have difficulties at the university.

6 **Read Study Skill** Find two examples of *however* in the article and circle them. What ideas does *however* contrast?

7 Match sentences 1–3 with sentences a–c. Rewrite them using *however*.

> 1 ☐ Some people think that 14 is too young for university.
> 2 ☐ Yinan Wang is only 14 years old.
> 3 ☐ At first Yinan Wang could only speak a little English.
>
> a He will soon be a student at Oxford University.
> b Now he is fluent in the language.
> c Others believe that clever students should not wait.

> **STUDY SKILL** Linking ideas (5)
>
> *However* is similar to *but*. We use *however* and *but* to contrast ideas. Look at sentences **a** and **b**. What differences are there?
>
> **a** *George studies hard at university.* **However**, *he never does well in exams.*
> **b** *George studies hard at university,* **but** *he never does well in exams.*

WRITING Formal letters and emails

1 Work with a partner. When do we write formal letters and emails?

applying for a job, ...

2 `Read Study Skill` Write formal greetings and endings for people 1–7.

> **STUDY SKILL** Greetings and endings
>
> Look at the ways of beginning and ending formal letters (and emails) in British English.
> **a** Greeting *Dear* (title and family name),
>   Ending *Yours sincerely,*
> **b** Greeting *Dear Sir/Madam,*
>   Ending *Yours faithfully,*

1 Miss Nancy Allen   *Dear Miss Allen ... Yours sincerely, ...*
2 The Manager, Human Resources
3 Mrs Helen Thomson
4 Mr Peter Ericson
5 Chairman, Department of Modern Languages
6 Dr Saeed Darwish
7 Ms Yoshiko Yamamoto

3 You are writing to Global Institute to request some information. Complete the email message using words in the box. `Read Study Skill`

have	hearing	would	information	sincerely	interested
please	know	studying	old	diploma	Dear

From:
Date: Wed, 27 Apr. 20:07:36 +0100 (BST)
To: "Global Institute" <globalinstitute@gi.net>
Subject: Information

¹_____ Mrs Fernandez,

I am ²_____ in ³_____English language and accounting at Global Institute. Could you ⁴_____ send me ⁵_____ about these courses? I ⁶_____ also like to ⁷_____ the starting dates of the next courses.

I am 21 years ⁸_____ and I am a manager in a hotel. I ⁹_____ a school leaving certificate and a ¹⁰_____ in hotel management.

I look forward to ¹¹_____ from you.

Yours ¹²_____,

> **STUDY SKILL** Words and phrases (2)
>
> **Language for letters and emails**
> Learn words and phrases to use in formal letters or emails.
>
> - **To ask for information/details/a form, etc.**
>   *I am interested in ... (studying/applying for) ...*
>   *I am writing to ask for ...*
>   *Could I have ...?*
>   *I would like to have/know ...*
>   *Could you please send me/attach (details of/information about) ...?*
> - **To give personal details**
>   *At the moment I am (studying/working) ...*
>   *I have a (degree/certificate/diploma) in ...*
> - **To close the letter/email**
>   *Thank you for ... (your help/time).*
>   *I look forward to (hearing/receiving/meeting) ...*

Dear Sir

Hi Zara!

Dear Madam

Hello Tom!

Dear Dr Patel

Yours faithfully

Yours sincerely

Bye!

4 Scan the advertisement for International Education College. Answer the questions.

- Where is the college?
- Can you study part-time?
- Can you apply online?
- Which subject interests you most?

International Education College

Come and study with us at **International Education College** (IEC). You can take undergraduate or postgraduate courses. You can study for degrees, diplomas, and certificates, full or part-time. Here are some of in the subjects we offer:

- Academic English
- Biological Sciences and the Environment
- Business
- Computing and IT
- Health and Sports Sciences
- Law
- Social Sciences
- Teaching and Education

Remember – your future is in your hands!

Come and join us!

For more information and an application form, write to us at: International Admissions Office, IEC, P.O. Box 5234, Sydney, Australia, **or email:** admissionsiec@iecuniv.ac.au

Writing a letter or email

5 Write a letter or email to the Admissions Office at IEC.

- Tell them which course you are interested in studying.
- Ask for an application form.
- Ask about applying online.
- Include personal details.

VOCABULARY DEVELOPMENT Spelling (2)

1 Read and match the rules.

2 Complete the table with the plurals of the nouns in the box. Use the rules and your dictionaries to help.

magazine	dictionary	fax	woman	city	email	address
bookshelf	company	day	virus	hobby	match	knife

-s	magazines
-es	
-ies	
irregular plurals	

RULES Plurals

Look at the countable nouns and their plurals. Match groups of words **1–4** with spelling rules **a–d**.

1 *student/students, boy/boys, office/offices*
2 *country/countries, company/companies, university/ universities*
3 *watch/watches, class/classes, box/boxes*
4 *mouse/mice, woman/women, child/children*

a nouns ending in consonant + *y*: change *-y* to *-ies*
b nouns ending in *-ch, -sh, -ss, -x*, or *-s*: add *-es*
c some nouns have irregular forms
d most nouns add *-s*

RESEARCH Notes

1 Think of four reasons for making notes? (See Study Skill p22.)
Notes help you:

<u>understand what you read, ...</u>

2 [Read Study Skill] Match the ways of making notes a–d from the Study Skill box with examples of students' notes 1–4.

STUDY SKILL Making notes (2)

There are many ways of making notes:
a making a list of points
b using diagrams and arrows
c <u>underlining</u> or highlighting words in the text (use coloured pens)
d making notes in margins of books or articles

1

Tower House of Yemen

The Tower Houses of Yemen are located in the old city of Sana'a, the capital of Yemen. ... They were built by local builders and they are hundreds of years old. They are made of stone and brick.

2

Measuring hurricanes.

Cat 1 – weakest winds 119– 153km/hour

We measure hurricanes by categories – from 1 to 5. A Category 1 hurricane is the weakest. It has winds of between 119 and 153 kms per hour. A Category 5

4

Ways of reading

– study/intensive reading

– skimming (for information)

– scanning (for general meaning)

3

<u>Applying to university</u>

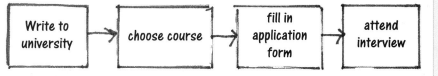

Write to university → choose course → fill in application form → attend interview

3 Look at the text about Moscow State University. What information is highlighted?

> **Moscow State University** is one of the most famous universities in the world. It was opened in 1755 and is more than 250 years old. The main building is on Sparrow Hills overlooking the Moscow River. The building has 36 floors and is 240 metres high. It was once the tallest building in Europe. The total number of undergraduate students is now about 40,000 and postgraduate students number about 7,000. There are also 9,000 professors, teachers, and researchers. In 1755 Moscow State University had only three faculties. Today it has 27 faculties. These are Mechanics and Mathematics, Physics, Chemistry, Geology, ...

4 Read about Harvard. Underline or highlight important information.

> **Harvard University** is a private university in Cambridge, Massachusetts in the USA. It is one of the world's most famous universities. It was founded in 1636 and is the oldest higher education institution in the USA. At first it was called the New College, but in 1696 it was named Harvard College after John Harvard. He gave money and books to the college. It became Harvard University, in 1780. Today Harvard University has about 2,300 professors. The number of undergraduate students is 6,650 and there are about 13,000 graduate students. It has nine faculties. These are Arts and Sciences, Law, Business, Medicine, ...

5 Find information about a college/university. Make highlighted notes. Work with a partner. Use your notes to talk about the college/university.

REVIEW

1 Complete the table with the plurals of the words in the box in the table.

> university   child   professor   genius   wife   faculty
> campus   family   friend   class   woman   building

-s	-es	-ies	irregular plurals
_____	_____	_____	_____
_____	_____	_____	_____
_____	_____	_____	_____

2 Match sentences 1–6 with a–f and then rewrite them using *however*.

Peter likes Global Institute. However, he doesn't like his course and wants to change it.

1 [d] Peter likes Global Institute.
2 [ ] Canada is one of the biggest countries in the world.
3 [ ] Pilots get good salaries.
4 [ ] Nancy is an excellent cook.
5 [ ] The sun is a good source of vitamin D.
6 [ ] Cars are an important part of modern life.

a They have to spend a lot of time away from home.
b Too much can cause skin cancer.
c They cause a lot of pollution.
d ~~He doesn't like his course and wants to change it.~~
e She usually prefers to eat in the canteen.
f It has a very small population.

3 Read the letter to Antonio Delgado at the Economics Academy. Correct the underlined mistakes. Add the missing words (⋏).

Dear Mr ⋏,

I am writing to <u>asking</u> for information <u>in</u> courses at the Economics Academy.
My name ⋏ Kemal Alpay. I am 19 years old and I live <u>to</u> Istanbul. I left school a
year ago and I am <u>work</u> in a hotel as an Assistant Manager.

I am <u>interesting</u> in the courses in business administration and economics.
Could ⋏ please send me <u>informations</u> about the courses?
I would also like to <u>now</u> when the next semester begins.

I look forward to <u>hear</u> from you.

<u>Your</u> sincerely,

Kemal Alpay

4 Work with a partner to complete the diagrams.

5 Compare your completed diagrams with the rest of the class.

6 Technology

READING SKILLS Getting information from websites • Using visuals in a website
WRITING SKILLS Writing definitions • Giving examples • Writing a description of a device
VOCABULARY DEVELOPMENT Homophones
RESEARCH Websites

READING Inventions

1 Match the inventions with the pictures.

> ☐ television ☐ the computer ☐ the printing press ☐ the washing machine
> ☐ the telephone ☐ the Internet ☐ the car ☐ the aeroplane ☐ radio ☐ satellites

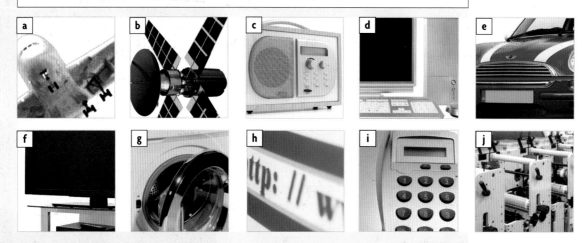

2 Which are the three most important inventions in exercise 1? Can you think of other important inventions? Discuss with a partner.

a 1st _____   b 2nd _____   c 3rd _____

3 Read the definition and examples.

An invention is a thing that someone has made for the first time, for example the telephone, or the computer.

Write a similar definition for *device* (tool for doing special jobs).
Give two examples.

A device is ...

4 ▌Read Study Skill▐ Scan the website article *Lost? Never again!* What do the letters *GPS* mean?

5 Skim the article. Match the headings a–d with paragraphs 1–4.

a ☐ When did the system start? c ☐ What is GPS?
b ☐ What is the future? d ☐ How does it work?

6 ▌Read Study Skill▐ Read paragraph 2 carefully. Complete the diagram with words from the box.

> ☐ ground station ☐ satellite ☐ receiver ☐ radio signal

STUDY SKILL Getting information from websites

Websites usually contain a lot of information. Some of the information is useful and some is not. Sometimes the language of a website is very technical and difficult to understand.

Use skimming and scanning skills to find the information you need.

STUDY SKILL Using visuals in a website

A website about a machine, a device, or a process usually has visuals. Study these diagrams and pictures. They give you extra information. They also help you understand how things work.

Lost? Never again!

Imagine the situation. You are driving alone in a desert or on a mountain. You have no idea where you are. You passed the last house two hours ago. Then your car breaks down. It is night and it is cold. You have no mobile phone. What do you do?

Well, next time take a GPS with you. This invention may be able to help you. It is a device which uses satellites to locate the user's position. It can <u>locate</u> your position to within 20 metres. Some GPS devices are even more accurate. A GPS cannot start your car, but at least you will know where you are.

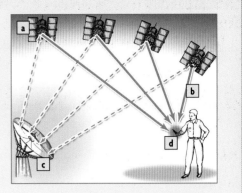

---

1 [_____]

GPS, which means Global Positioning System, is a small <u>portable</u> radio receiver. It looks like a mobile phone. You can hold it in your hand, or put in your pocket. It is sometimes fitted into a watch or a telephone. We also find GPS devices in cars, aeroplanes, or boats. Some of these devices, for example the Garmin GPSMAP 60, have electronic maps, so you know exactly where you are. For example, in a city they can tell you the name of the street.

2 [_____]

There are three parts to the Global Positioning System. The first part is the receiver. You can hold it in your hand, or have it fixed into your car, plane, etc. The second part is a group of satellites <u>orbiting</u> the Earth. The satellites carry atomic clocks and transmit radio signals. The receiver contacts at least four of the satellites. It measures the distance from each satellite, using the radio waves and the times. The receiver then <u>calculates</u> its exact position. The third part of the system is a network of ground stations. They are located all over the world. They control the satellites and make sure they are working well.

3 [_____]

The United States Department of Defense designed the system for the military. They <u>launched</u> the first satellite into space in 1978. In the 1980s the government made the system available to everyone – for free. By 1998 there were 24 satellites in orbit around the world. When a satellite becomes old or breaks down, a new satellite is sent up in its place.

4 [_____]

Some people think that in the future the GPS will be as common as the mobile. They are becoming cheaper and more and more <u>accurate</u>. There are also new uses for the GPS, such as <u>tracking</u> criminals. Perhaps they will become like watches. Everyone will have one and you will never be lost again!

---

7 Match the underlined words in the text with definitions 1–7.

1 sent up into space _____
2 finds the answer by using mathematics _____
3 that you can move or carry easily _____
4 following signs or marks to find somebody _____
5 exactly right, with no mistakes _____
6 moving round something in space _____
7 find the exact position of something _____

WRITING Describing things

1 **Read Study Skill** Read definitions 1–4. Circle *which* or *that*, and underline the clauses.

1. A thermometer is **an instrument** which measures temperature.
2. A satellite is **an object** that circles another object.
3. A vacuum cleaner is **a machine** which cleans carpets.
4. A laptop is **a type of computer** that is portable and weighs about 1–3kg.

2 Match the two parts of the sentences to make definitions for the objects. Use *which* or *that*.

1	A photocopier is a machine	a	... is made by Apple.
2	A remote control is a device	b	... controls things, such as televisions, from a distance.
3	A drill is a tool	c	... makes copies of documents, such as letters.
4	A speedometer is an instrument	d	... you use for making holes.
5	An iPod is a type of MP3 player	e	... tells you how fast you are travelling in a car or a plane.

3 Complete the definitions in the same way.

1. A calculator is an instrument …
2. A fax machine is a machine …
3. A microwave is a type of oven …
4. A laser …

4 **Read Study Skill** Find three ways of giving examples in the website on GPS. There are two in paragraph 1 and one in paragraph 4.

> **STUDY SKILL** Giving examples
>
> When you describe an object or give a definition, you usually give examples. Look at the ways of giving examples **a–c**. How are they different?
>
> **a** *Mobile phone companies,* **such as** *Nokia and Motorola, are very successful.*
> **b** *Planets orbit the sun, but other bodies orbit the planets.* **For example**, *the moon, orbits the Earth.*
> **c** *There are many planets in our solar system,* **for example** *Mars, Jupiter, and the Earth.*
>
> We can use the abbreviation *e.g.* instead of *for example*.
> *There are many planets in our solar system,* **e.g.** *Mars, Jupiter, and the Earth.*

5 Complete the example sentences.

1. There are many different makes of television, for example _____ .
2. A GPS has many uses. For example, we _____ .
3. We cannot live without modern inventions, such as _____ , because they are a part of our way of life.
4. There are many types of sports car, _____ .

6 Read about laptops. Complete the paragraph with the words in the box.

| so | such as | type | but | because | which | example |

Laptops are a ¹_____ of personal computer ²_____ you can use anywhere. They are also known as a notebook computer, for ³_____ the IBM Thinkpad. Laptops usually weigh between one and three kilograms, ⁴_____ they are easy to carry around. These computers can run on batteries, ⁵_____ they can also use mains electricity. Laptops are becoming very popular ⁶_____ they are cheaper than before. You can use them in different places, ⁷_____ libraries, canteens, on a train, or even in the street. They are useful for businessmen and women, and also for students.

Writing a description of a device

7 Find information about one of these modern devices (or choose your own) and make notes.

| digital cameras | bluetooth | mobile phones | DVD players | compact discs | Segway | MP3 players |

8 Read about laptops in exercise 6 again. Use your notes about a device from exercise 7 to write a similar paragraph (50–80 words). Include a definition and examples.

9 Read about satellites. Correct the spelling and grammar mistakes.

A satellite is any object <u>wich</u> orbits another object. All bodies that <u>is</u> part of the solar system, for <u>exampel</u> the Earth and Jupiter, are <u>satelites</u>. Most ⋏ these bodies orbit the sun, but others orbit planets. For example, the moon <u>orbit</u> the Earth. When we <u>using</u> the term 'satellite', we <u>usual</u> mean an artificial satellite. This ⋏ a man-made <u>objict</u> that orbits the Earth, or <u>an other</u> body. However, <u>sceintists</u> may also use the term for natural satellites, or moons.

10 Read your paragraph from exercise 8 again. Check your spelling, punctuation, and grammar.

VOCABULARY DEVELOPMENT Spelling (3)

Read Study Skill Complete the sentences with the words in brackets.

1 The mechanic doesn't _____ how to fix the car, and I have _____ idea.(*no/know*)

2 I like autumn. _____ the best season in my country. (*it's/its*)

3 I think that fourteen is _____ young for a child _____ go to university. (*to/too*)

4 _____ are a lot of mistakes in _____ report. _____ writing it again. (*they're/there/their*)

RESEARCH Websites

1 **Read Study Skill** Look at the three examples of websites. They are all about wind power. Answer the questions.

1 Label the web pages. Which is … ?
- a company website
- an online encyclopaedia entry
- someone's personal page

2 Which is best for researching an essay on wind power? Why?

a

WIKIPEDIA
The Free Encyclopedia

| article | discussion | edit this page | history |

navigation
- Main Page
- Community Portal
- Current events
- Recent changes
- Random article
- Contact Wikipedia
- Donations

search

[Go] [Search]

Wind power
From Wikipedia, the free encyclopedia

Wind power is the conversion of wind energy into more useful forms, usually electricity using wind turbines. In 2005, worldwide capacity of wind-powered generators was 58,982 megawatts, their production making up less than 1% of world-wide electricity use. Although still a relatively minor source of electricity for most countries, it accounts for 23% of electricity use in Denmark, 4.3% in Germany and around 8% in Spain. Globally, wind power generation more than quadrupled between 1999 and 2005.

b

North
Energy.co.uk

GAZELLE WIND TURBINES
The Gazelle is manufactured by Gazelle Wind Turbines Ltd, a member of the the MKW group, at:

Wentworth Ind Est
Wolvercot
Manchester
M40 3EX

For sales and information contact Tom Chaplin on:
0161 496 0731
email: tChaplin.Gazelle@mkw.net
website: www.mkw.co.uk

c

Illustrated History of Wind Power Development

The historical and technical information in this section is derived from many sources. Information on developments since 1975 is based primarily on my personal experience with the U.S. Federal Wind Energy Program, my extensive reading (and editing) of wind energy journals and research reports over the last 25 years, my conversations with wind energy researchers, interactions with members of the wind energy community, and my personal view of wind power developments and of the wind industry. Opinions expressed here are my own, of course.

2 Choose one of the topics from the box.

| paper | four-wheel drive cars | silk | handbags |
| paper clips | contact lenses | plastic | water filters |

1 Find three websites with information about the topic.
2 Decide if the websites are useful or not useful for writing a report.
3 Explain your reasons to other students in the class.

REVIEW

1 Put the words in order to make definitions.

Gold is a metal …

1 to / metal / used / jewellery / is / gold / make / a / which
2 clothes / a / washes / washing machine / that / is / machine
3 lives / a / an / is / large / Africa / elephant / which / in / animal / very
4 causes / storm / a / damage / that / a lot of / is / hurricane / a / tropical
5 a kind of / is / that / like / a / person / robot / works / a / machine

2 Complete the table with inventions from the box. Are they forms of transport, for work and study, or the home? Then add other inventions to the table.

| the metro | a fax machine | a washing machine | an aeroplane |
| a train | a dishwasher | a microwave | a photocopier | a printer |

transport	work/study	home
the metro		

3 Use the words in the box to complete the sentences. The words are all from Unit 6.

| calculate | distance | accurate | locate | device |
| network | lost | portable | exactly | launch |

1 You can carry it easily in your pocket. It is _____.
2 I don't know where we are. We are completely _____.
3 My watch is not very _____. It is ten minutes slow at the moment.
4 How can you _____ the average age of people in the class?
5 They use rockets to _____ the satellites into space.
6 I know _____ where we are. We are here – on this street.
7 The World Wide Web is an international _____ of computers.
8 What's the _____ from your home to the college?
9 A tin-opener is a very simple _____ , but a very important one.
10 In the past, sailors and travellers used the sun and the stars to _____ their position.

7 Food, drink, and culture

READING SKILLS Topic sentences • Writer's opinion
WRITING SKILLS Punctuation (2) • Linking ideas (6) • Using pronouns • Writing about food and drink
VOCABULARY DEVELOPMENT Prefixes

READING Food from other countries

	local	outside
rice		
flour		
sugar		
tea		
coffee		
apples		
strawberries		
tomatoes		
potatoes		
lamb		

1 In your country, where do the food items in the table come from? Are they mainly local, do they come from outside your country, or both? Discuss in groups. Write ✓ or ✗ to complete the table.

2 Look at the title of the article and the map on p41. Answer the questions.

   1 What do you think 'food mile' means?
   2 What information will you find in the article?
   3 Which five words will you find? Choose from the box.

> teacher   farmer   tennis   market   television   satellite
> fresh   book   aeroplanes   happy   distance   cup   watch

3 Scan the article quickly. Find a definition for *food mile* and underline it.

4 **Read Study Skill** Skim the article and match the topic sentences a–e with paragraphs 1–4. There is one extra topic sentence.

  a ☐ What is wrong with a lot of food miles?
  b ☐ Traditionally, farmers sold their food in the local market, so the food did not have to travel very far.
  c ☐ Nowadays, the food that you buy comes from many different countries.
  d ☐ Tomatoes are not tasty nowadays because of food miles.
  e ☐ Some countries have to import most of their food.

STUDY SKILL Topic sentences

A topic sentence tells you what a paragraph is about. It is usually the first sentence in a paragraph. It is important to identify topic sentences. They help you read and understand a text more quickly.

5 Read the sentences from the article. What do you think the underlined words mean? Use the context to help.

Check the <u>origins</u> of the food. Perhaps there are apples from California, lamb from New Zealand, or potatoes from Egypt?

<u>Origins</u> means the places where the food comes from.

  1 A food mile is the distance that food travels from the farmer's field to the person who buys the food. Nowadays, food often travels thousands of miles to get to the <u>consumer</u>.
  2 This was a good system for farmers and consumers. However, there were some <u>disadvantages</u>.
  3 We do not have to wait for spring or summer to buy strawberries or tomatoes. They are <u>available</u> in winter if we want.
  4 The United Arab Emirates (UAE), for example, gets 85% of its food from other countries. Even food made in the UAE often uses <u>imported</u> materials.

6 Which sentence shows the writer's opinion on food miles?
  Read Study Skill

  1 Food miles are useful for international trade.
  2 It is good that we can eat strawberries in winter.
  3 Long journeys by food cause pollution and global warming.

STUDY SKILL Writer's opinion

You can usually find out the writer's opinion if you read carefully. A good writer gives both sides of an argument, but also has an opinion.

Food miles: from field to plate

1 ⬚ Have a look in your fridge, cupboard, and fruit bowl and check the origins of the food. Perhaps there are apples from California, lamb from New Zealand, or potatoes from Egypt? You will probably be surprised how far food travels to get to your plate. This journey, from 'field to plate', is called 'food miles'. A food mile is the distance that food travels from the farmer's field to the person who buys the food. Nowadays, food often travels thousands of miles to get to the consumer. Why is this, and what are the effects of these long distances?

2 ⬚ The consumers also did not travel very far because they went to their local market to buy the food. This was a good system for farmers and consumers. However, there were some disadvantages. For example, consumers could only buy food that farmers produced locally. In addition, they could only get food that was in season. Now, because of modern technology, food comes from all over the world. We do not have to wait for spring or summer to buy strawberries or tomatoes. They are available in winter if we want.

3 ⬚ This is because they have difficult climates. The United Arab Emirates (UAE), for example, gets 85% of its food from other countries. Even food made in the UAE often uses imported materials. An example is a type of bread called Tasty Loaf, which is made locally. Tasty Loaf contains ingredients such as flour and sugar from Australia, Germany, China, Malaysia, and India. If we add up all the distances, one loaf of this bread (about 450 grams) requires a total of 12,690 kilometres. This is a lot of 'food miles'.

4 ⬚ Is this not a good way of increasing international trade? I believe these miles are worrying for a number of reasons. First of all, because food travels such long distances, we need more aeroplanes, lorries, and ships to move the food. This means we use more oil or petrol, so there is more pollution and more global warming. In addition, food that travels a long way is not fresh and usually not very tasty. Tomatoes, for example, are picked early and stored for their long journeys. For this reason, they are usually tasteless when they get to the consumer. Local food has a better taste, and it also reduces the amount of global pollution. We need to buy more local food.

7 Complete the summary of the article using the words in the box.

disadvantage	because	imported	petrol	consumer
local	pollution	season	distance	nowadays

Summary

A 'food mile' is the [1]_____ that food travels from the farmer's field to the [2]_____. In the past, people went to their [3]_____ market to buy food. One [4]_____ was that they could only buy food that was in [5]_____, for example tomatoes in the summer. [6]_____, however, we can send food around the world and we can eat any food at any time of the year. Some countries, such as the UAE, use a lot of [7]_____ food because they have difficult climates. Food miles are a problem [8]_____ we use more oil and [9]_____. This causes [10]_____ and global warming.

WRITING Describing food and drink

1 `Read Study Skill` Punctuate the sentences with commas.

> ## STUDY SKILL Punctuation (2)
>
> Look at the sentences. Circle the commas.
>
> *Tasty Loaf contains ingredients such as flour and sugar from Australia, Germany, China, Malaysia, and India.*
>
> Use commas to separate the things in the list. You can put a comma before *and*.

1 Danny's favourite foods are pizza chocolate burgers and ice-cream.
2 The three materials used in the building were glass concrete and steel.
3 Parwin speaks five languages fluently: Farsi English Urdu Turkish and French.
4 For the experiment you will need water salt a bowl and a small piece of paper.
5 The ingredients of a Spanish omelette are onions eggs potatoes and salt.

2 `Read Study Skill` Match sentences 1–4 with a–d. Rewrite them using *In addition*.

> ## STUDY SKILL Linking ideas (6)
>
> We use *In addition* and *and* to join two similar ideas, or to add extra information. *In addition* is like *and* in meaning, but it is more formal.
>
> Look at sentences **a** and **b**. How is the punctuation different?
> **a** *George studies hard at university.* **In addition**, *he has a part-time job in a hotel.*
> **b** *George studies hard at university,* **and** *he has a part-time job in a hotel.*
>
> Underline two examples of *In addition* in the article, and circle the commas.

Lebanese food is delicious. It is very healthy.
Lebanese food is delicious. In addition, it is very healthy.

1 ☐ Aeroplanes cause a lot of air pollution.	a	There is very little rainfall.
2 ☐ Food that travels a long distance is not very fresh.	b	The food is usually cheaper than in supermarkets.
3 ☐ Shopping in local markets is more interesting.	c	They make a lot of noise when they land and take off.
4 ☐ The climate is very hot in Saudi Arabia.	d	It is very expensive because of the costs of transport

3 Read sentences a–f from a paragraph on food and culture.

1 Find the topic sentence for the paragraph.
2 Put the sentences in the correct order 1–6 to make a paragraph. Start with the topic sentence.

Food, drink, and culture

a ☐ It can be as important as language, music, or literature.

b ☐ In addition, drinks can also be important to a culture.

c ☐ Eating rice, for example, is central to the culture of China.

d ☐ For example, mint tea is a traditional part of daily life for people in Morocco.

e ☐ Food is an important part of any culture.

f ☐ Similarly, the Italian way of life would be very different without pasta.

4 **Read Study Skill** Replace the underlined noun in each sentence with a pronoun from the box.

she	it	they	his	her	them

1 The car broke down in the middle of the desert. It was impossible to repair <u>the car</u>.
2 You can buy strawberries at any time of the year. However, some people prefer to buy <u>strawberries</u> in season.
3 Students work very hard on this course. <u>Students</u> write five projects every semester.
4 My brother is very upset at the moment. <u>My brother's</u> exam results were not very good.
5 My sister is happy with the new job. <u>My sister's</u> salary is better than before and <u>my sister</u> has longer holidays.

> **STUDY SKILL** Using pronouns
>
> We use pronouns (*I, me, he, him, it, them, they*, etc.) to avoid repeating a noun. It makes our writing easier to read. For example:
>
> *Tomatoes are picked early and stored for **their** long journeys. **They** are usually tasteless when **they** get to the consumer. Local food has a better taste, and **it** also reduces global pollution.*

5 Read the paragraph about Moroccan tea. Underline the topic sentence. Add the pronouns *they, it,* or *them* to the paragraph.

The most important drink in Morocco is mint tea. ¹_____ is really a part of Moroccan culture. People can drink this tea at any time of the day, but in most homes ²_____ usually have ³_____ after meals. They make the tea using green tea leaves, which they put into a special teapot. Then they take some fresh mint leaves and add ⁴_____ to the teapot. They add boiling water and lots of sugar. After a few minutes, they pour the tea into small glasses and they place ⁵_____ on a tray. Finally, they serve the tea. ⁶_____ is delicious on a hot day.

Writing about food and drink

6 What is the most important food or drink in your culture? Write a paragraph for a foreign visitor. Use a topic sentence to begin your paragraph, for example:

The most important food/drink in … is …

VOCABULARY DEVELOPMENT Prefixes and their meanings

1 ▨ **Read Study Skill** Use a dictionary to complete the definition of *prefix*.

A prefix is a group of letters that . . .

> ### STUDY SKILL Prefixes
>
> Use prefixes to help you understand the meaning of a word.
> Some prefixes give a word the opposite meaning. For example:
> - **dis-** gives the noun *advantages* the opposite meaning:
>   *However, there were some **dis**advantages.*
> - **un-** gives the adjective *helpful* the opposite meaning:
>   *The people were very **un**helpful.*
>
> Look at these other prefixes and their meanings.
> **anti-** (against) – *anticlockwise*
> **sub-** (under) – *subway*
> **super-** (above, large) – *supervisor, supermarket*
> **pre-** (before) – *predict*
> **multi-** (many) – *multimedia*

anti-

sub-

super-

pre-

multi-

2 Match the underlined words in 1–6 with meanings a–f.

1	☐ Most drivers are <u>impatient</u> when they are at the traffic lights.	a	does not happen often
2	☐ I <u>distrust</u> most advertisements.	b	different opinions
3	☐ I want to buy an <u>inexpensive</u> watch. I haven't got much money.	c	cheap
4	☐ It was <u>irresponsible</u> to let the children play in the busy street.	d	not wanting to wait for something
5	☐ It is <u>unusual</u> to have so much rain in the desert.	e	not sensible
6	☐ Yuki and Toni had a <u>disagreement</u>. Now they are not speaking to each other.	f	do not believe

3 Add the negative prefixes in the box to the words in the sentences. Use a dictionary to help you.

> un-   in-   ir-   im-   dis-

1 Kim felt very ___happy when he saw the exam results.
2 Paulo ___liked the new lecturer. He thought her lectures were difficult to understand.
3 It is difficult to learn all the ___regular verbs in English.
4 This exercise is ___possible. I can't do it.
5 The essay is ___complete. You must write a conclusion.
6 It is ___moral to take money from the poor.
7 Because the statistics were ___accurate, we had to calculate the results again.
8 Rafa is a very ___organized person. His desk is always ___tidy and he's usually late for meetings.

un-

in-

ir-

im-

dis-

4 Match the underlined words 1–5 with meanings a–e.

1	☐ You should <u>preview</u> the document and then print it.	a	medicine for curing infection
2	☐ After the success of her TV show, Belal became a <u>superstar</u> in her own country.	b	with many floors
3	☐ The film was in English, but fortunately there were <u>subtitles</u>.	c	words at the bottom of a film/TV screen to help you understand
4	☐ The <u>antibiotic</u> penicillin was discovered in 1928.	d	a very famous singer or actor
5	☐ The city centre has a <u>multi-storey</u> car park.	e	see before

REVIEW

1 Complete the words from Unit 7 with two vowels.

1 ingred _ _ nts	5 ar _ _ nd	9 f _ _ ld
2 on _ _ ns	6 cont _ _ ns	10 b _ _ lding
3 m _ _ sure	7 c _ _ ntries	11 r _ _ son
4 s _ _ son	8 br _ _ d	12 mater _ _ ls

2 Skim the article about coffee and match the topic sentences with the paragraphs. There is one extra topic sentence.

a In many societies coffee is an important part of the culture.
b Coffee has a similar position in many western societies.
c Originally coffee came from Ethiopia, in Africa.
d Coffee is made from the roasted beans of the coffee plant.

Coffee

1 _____. The plant is grown in many different parts of the world, such as Brazil and Kenya. Coffee producers collect the green beans and roast them. The colour changes to brown and the beans become bigger. People then grind the beans into small grains. These are then boiled with water to produce coffee.

2 _____. It then spread to the Arabian peninsula. The word coffee, in fact, comes from the Arabic *qahwa*. Later, in the 16th century, it became popular in Turkey, where it was called kahve. It then spread to Italy and the rest of Europe.

3 _____. In Bedouin Arab society, for example, people make fresh coffee early in the morning. They heat the coffee pot on a wood fire and keep it hot all day. When guests arrive, the hosts offer them coffee in small cups. There is even a way of showing the host by a signal that you would like more, or you have had enough.

3 Find adjectives, nouns, and verbs with negative prefixes in Unit 7. Add them to the diagrams. Make sure your words are negatives (*dis*agree, not *dis*tance; *un*happy not *un*iversity).

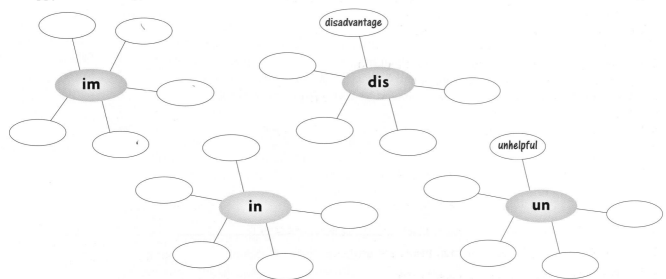

4 Use your dictionary to find other words to add to the diagram.

8 Cities of the world

READING SKILLS Looking at data • Getting facts from a text
WRITING SKILLS Comparatives and superlatives • Linking ideas (7) • Writing about cities
RESEARCH Finding facts and figures
VOCABULARY DEVELOPMENT Word-attack skills

READING City life

1 What things are important to you in a city? Put the following in order 1 to 5 (1 is the most important).

☐ climate ☐ transport ☐ education ☐ safety ☐ recreation

2 Which city in the world would you most like to live in? Give reasons.

3 [Read Study Skill] Scan the article *The world's best city* to find the information.

1 the name of the group that did the survey
2 the number of cities in the survey
3 the 'best' and the 'worst' cities
4 the top Asian cities

4 Look at the article again to complete the table *Top Ten Cities*.

5 Read the article. Answer the questions.

1 Where are famous cities like Paris, London, and New York in the table? What reasons does the writer give?
2 How do some African cities do? What reasons does the writer give?
3 Why do you think Japanese cities have high scores?
4 What do you think of surveys like this? Do you believe the results? Why/why not?

STUDY SKILL Looking at data

We often show data (or statistics) in tables, pie or bar charts, graphs, etc.

Year	Population
1970	12.3m
1980	12.7m
1990	12.9m
2000	13.3m
2010	13.6m

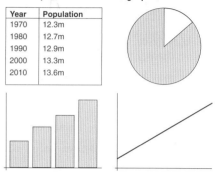

Study the information in visuals to help you understand a text.

The world's best city

Which is the best city in the world to live and work in? Every year the Economist Intelligence Unit asks this question. It uses factors such as climate, transport, education, safety, and recreational facilities for around 127 world cities. They give scores for each, and then rank the cities in order – from the 'best' to the 'worst'.

This year all of the top ten cities came from either Canada, Australia, or Western Europe. Vancouver, Canada had the highest score, which means it is the most 'liveable' city. Two other Canadian cities, Toronto (9th place) and Calgary (10th), were also in the top ten. In second place was Melbourne, Australia followed by Vienna (Austria), Geneva (Switzerland), and Perth (Australia).

At the bottom of the list were the cities with the most difficult or dangerous living conditions. The city with the lowest score was Port Moresby, Papua New Guinea in 127th place. Just above were Karachi, Pakistan, and Dhaka, Bangladesh. Some African cities, such as Lagos, Nigeria also did badly. This could be because of climate, or the political situation in these countries.

In the middle of the list came big cosmopolitan cities with their transport and crime problems. These included Paris (32nd), London (44th), and New York (52nd). The Japanese cities of Osaka and Tokyo did better, however. These cities (both 21st) also had the biggest scores in Asia.

TOP TEN CITIES	
1	_____
2	_____
3	_____
4	_____
5	_____
6	Adelaide
7	Sydney
8	Zurich
9	_____
10	_____

6 [Read Study Skill] Look at the webpage *Welcome to Vancouver*. Scan the text and visuals to answer the questions.

1 What ocean is the city on?
2 What is the temperature in the summer?
3 Is there snow in winter?
4 Which month is the wettest?
5 What is the total population?
6 What is the second language of the city after English?
7 How did the city get its name?
8 Where can you get a good view of the city?

STUDY SKILL Getting facts from a text

Remember – use headings in a text and the titles of visuals. They can help you find the information you want quickly.

Welcome to Vancouver
– Canada's Coolest City!

Location
Vancouver is located in the south-west corner of Canada, just to the north of the border with the United States. Vancouver is a busy port and tourist centre. It is situated on a peninsula and is surrounded by the Pacific Ocean on three sides. On the other side of the city are mountains, which rise to over 1500 metres.

Population
According to the 2001 census, the population of Vancouver City is about 540,000. However, there are more than two million people living in the region. The population is ethnically very mixed. The largest ethnic group is Chinese, although there are many Indians, Vietnamese, and Filipinos. Nearly a quarter of the population say that Chinese is their mother tongue. Only about half of the population speak English as their mother tongue.

History
Vancouver was founded as a small settlement called Granville in the 1870s. It was a small trading port for wood. In 1886 the city was renamed after a British naval captain, George Vancouver.

Climate
It has one of the mildest climates in Canada. The summers are usually sunny and dry. The hottest months are July and August. However, the temperature rarely goes above 22°C. The winter is mild. It is also the wettest season. There is some snow in the winter, but usually just on the mountains near the city.

Things to see
Vancouver is famous for its scenery. It has more than 180 parks, including the famous Stanley Park. Near the city are forests and snow-capped mountains. Sports include skiing, hiking, cycling, and boating. The most interesting sights include Gastown (the historic area of Vancouver), Chinatown, English Bay, Vancouver Harbour, and Robson Street, which is the main shopping street for high fashion. You can also take a trip to Granville Island, where you can buy paintings from artists' studios. To get a great panoramic view of Vancouver, visitors should go to the Lookout – a viewing platform at the top of the Harbour Centre Tower.

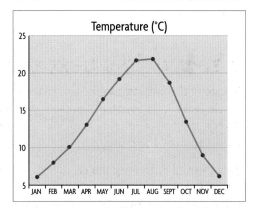

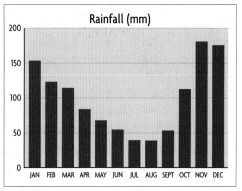

WRITING Comparing data

1 Look at the data about Toronto and Moscow. Say if the sentences are true (**T**)
or false (**F**).

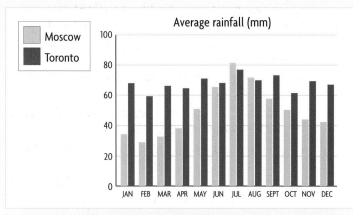
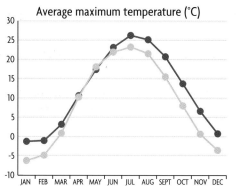

1 Toronto is wetter than Moscow in the winter.
2 Moscow is drier than Toronto in the spring.
3 August is the wettest month in Moscow.
4 February is the driest month in Toronto.
5 Moscow is hotter than Toronto in the summer.
6 Moscow is colder than Toronto in the winter.
7 June is the hottest month in Moscow.
8 January and February are the coldest months in Toronto.

2 Underline the comparative and superlative adjectives
in the sentences in exercise 1.

3 Read the rules. Write the comparative and superlative
form of the adjectives in the box.

| wet   beautiful   dry   cold   hot   friendly |
| popular   mild   difficult   cool   big   nice   low |

adjective	comparative	superlative
wet	wetter	the wettest
beautiful	more beautiful	the most beautiful

> **RULES** Comparatives and superlatives
>
> Study the spelling rules for comparatives and superlatives:
> a adjectives of one syllable, for example *high*, add *-er* and *-est*
> b adjectives ending in *-e*, for example *nice*, add only *-r* and *-st*
> c some adjectives, for example *big*, double the last letter
> d adjectives ending in *-y*, for example *dry*, change *-y* to *-i*
>
> Remember – long adjectives do not follow these rules. They
> use **more** and **most**, and **less** and **least**. For example:
>
> *Tokyo is **more expensive than** Paris.*
> ***The most interesting** sights include Gastown, Chinatown, …*

4 Look at the population statistics for three countries in Asia.
Complete the paragraph. Use the statistics from the table
and the adjectives in the box.

| high/low (birth rate)   small/big (population) |

	births (per 1000 population)	total population
Japan	9.37	127,463,611
China	13.25	1,313,973,713
South Korea	10	48,846,823

The table shows population statistics for three Asian
countries: Japan, China, and South Korea. China has the [1]_____ population, over 1.3
billion people. Japan's population is about [2]_____ million. This is less than South Korea's
population, which is just under [3]_____ million. South Korea has the [4]_____
population of these three countries. The country with the [5]_____ birth rate is China.
There are [6]_____ births per million population. Japan has the [7]_____ birth rate,
[8]_____ births per 1000. South Korea's birth rate is a little [9]_____ than Japan's,
but [10]_____ than China's.

5 Read Study Skill Underline the *which* and *where* clauses in the sentences. Circle the commas.

1 Melbourne, which is one of the largest cities in Australia, came second in the survey.

2 The highest-ranking cities in Asia were Osaka and Tokyo, which is the capital of Japan.

3 Chinatown, where there are many good restaurants, is located near the centre of the city.`

4 On Monday we visited the Grand Bazaar in Istanbul, where you can buy everything from carpets to gold chains.

STUDY SKILL Linking ideas (7)

Use relative pronouns *which* and *where* to add information about things (*which*) and places (*where*).
Look at sentences **a** and **b**. What are the differences? Underline the relative pronouns in **b**. Circle the comma.

a *On the other side of the city are mountains. **They** rise to over 1500 metres.*

b *On the other side of the city are mountains, **which** rise to over 1500 metres.*

Look at sentences **c** and **d**. What are the differences? Underline the relative pronouns in **d**. Circle the comma.

c *You can also take a trip to Granville Island. You can buy paintings from artists' studios **there**.*

d *You can also take a trip to Granville Island, **where** you can buy paintings from artists' studios.*

Writing about cities

6 Look at the notes about Mumbai. Complete the paragraph using the notes.

Name:	Mumbai (also Bombay)
Location:	west coast of India
Climate:	cool and dry in winter, hot in spring, wet in summer (monsoon season)
Population:	18 m (largest city in India)
Famous for:	film industry (Bollywood), port, commercial centre
History:	founded 1668 by British East India Company
Things to see:	Mani Bhavan Museum, Chowpatty beach
Source:	www.wikipedia.org

Mumbai – India's largest city

Mumbai, which is also known as ¹_____, lies on the ²_____ coast of India. The best time to visit is during the months of December, January, and February. The spring is very ³_____ and the summers are wet because this is the ⁴_____ season. The city has a population of ⁵_____ people. It is famous for its very successful ⁶_____ industry and its port. It is also an important commercial centre. The city was founded in ⁷_____ by the ⁸_____ Company. There are many sights to see in Mumbai, including the Mani Bhavan ⁹_____, and the famous Chowpatty beach.

7 Rewrite the text about Mumbai. Include *which* and *where* clauses a–d to add information. Use commas where necessary.

a which is called Bollywood

b where the people of Mumbai like to walk in the evenings

c which are usually cool and dry

d which makes it the largest city in India

RESEARCH Researching a city

1 [Read Study Skill] Choose a city you would like to visit.
Find out information about it. Give the source (or sources).
Make notes.

STUDY SKILL Finding facts and figures

Make a note of good sources of facts and figures – about
cities, countries, climate, people, etc. They will help you in
your studies. Here are some useful websites to begin with:

www.worldfactsandfigures.com

www.wikipedia.org

encarta.msn.com

Name: _____

Location: _____

Climate: _____

Population: _____

Famous for: _____

History: _____

Things to see: _____

Source: _____

2 Use your notes from exercise 1 to write a paragraph about the city for visitors.
Look again at the paragraph about Mumbai on page 49 to help.

VOCABULARY DEVELOPMENT New words

[Read Study Skill] Use word-attack skills on the words in bold.

STUDY SKILL Word-attack skills on new words

Sometimes the different parts of a word can help you guess the meaning.

Look at the word *liveable* in this sentence:

*Vancouver, Canada had the highest score,
which means it is the most **liveable** city.*

Look at the two parts:
live/able

■ *live* is a verb   ■ *-able* means you can

So *liveable* is an adjective meaning *you can
live there*.

Look at the word *renamed* in this sentence:

*In 1886 the city was **renamed** after a British
naval captain George Vancouver.*

Look at the three parts:
re/name/d

■ *re-*   ■ *name*   ■ *-d*

What does *renamed* mean?

1 Many nouns such as *time*, *air*, *water*, and *information* are **uncountable**.
2 If you fail the exam, you will have to **retake** it next semester.
3 Belal is a very **disorganized** person. She is late for lessons and always forgets
her books.
4 After the fire, they **rebuilt** the school.
5 The city was **unrecognizable** – it had changed so much.

REVIEW

1 How many ways are there to show data? Add words to the diagram.

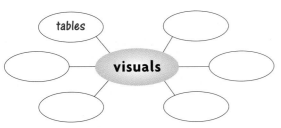

2 Match the sentences 1–5 with sentences a–e. Use *which* to make clauses.
Use the correct punctuation.

1 ☐ New York is the best-known city in North America.	a They are located near the centre of the city.
2 ☐ Port Moresby has a very high crime rate.	b It is the main shopping street for fashion.
3 ☐ In Vancouver you can go skiing in the mountains.	c They surround the city and are covered in snow in the winter.
4 ☐ Robson Street is well worth a visit.	d It is the capital of Papua New Guinea.
5 ☐ London is famous for its beautiful parks.	e It is located on Manhattan Island.

3 Complete the *where* clauses using your own words.

1 In summer many people go to the mountains, where _____ .
2 In the centre of the city is the main square, where _____ .
.3 The National Stadium, where_____ , is located near the station.
4 Near the harbour there are many restaurants, where_____ .
5 There is a river in the middle of the city, where _____ .

4 Look at the table. Write five sentences about the information.

The birth rate in Turkey is higher than in Russia and Germany.

	Turkey	Russia	Germany
births (per 1000 population)	18.31	9.35	9.16
total population	66,493,970	145,470,197	83,029,536

5 Find the information as quickly as you can to complete the *City Quiz*.

CITY QUIZ

1 Which is the world's largest city?

2 What is its population (latest figure)?

3 Which city is wetter?
   a Rio de Janeiro   b Lisbon

4 Which city is not located by the sea?
   a Istanbul   d Berlin
   b Shanghai   e Karachi
   c Manila   f Cape Town

5 In which city can you find…?
   a the Prado Museum
   b Shalimar Gardens
   c the Golden Gate Bridge

6 Which city is the oldest?
   a Damascus
   b Mexico City
   c St Petersburg

7 Which city is the highest above
   sea level?
   a Delhi
   b Nairobi
   c Riyadh

8 Only one of these cities is a capital
   city. Which one?
   a New York   d Bangkok
   b Sydney   e Amsterdam
   c Rio de Janeiro f Mumbai

9 Brain power

READING SKILLS In other words • Making notes (3)
WRITING SKILLS Common mistakes • Summaries • Writing a summary
RESEARCH Books

READING A healthy brain

1 What do you know about the human brain? Answer the questions in the *Brain Quiz* on page 53.

2 Scan the information in *Brain facts* on page 53 to check your answers.

3 Skim the article *How to keep your brain healthy*. Match topic sentences a–e with paragraphs 1–5.

- a ☐ Physical activity is also important.
- b ☐ Finally, we should eat a 'brain-healthy' diet.
- c ☐ Another thing we can do is to be socially active.
- d ☐ 1 Most people know how to keep their bodies healthy.
- e ☐ First of all, it is important to stay mentally active

4 **Read Study Skill** Look at the underlined words and phrases in the article. Find synonyms in the same paragraph.

- a exercise (paragraph 2) _____
- b socialize (paragraph 3) _____
- c beneficial (paragraph 4) _____
- d avoid (paragraph 5) _____
- e nutritious (paragraph 5) _____
- f improve brainpower (paragraph 5) _____

STUDY SKILL In other words

Sometimes writers do not want to repeat words. It is not good style. They use pronouns (*it*, *he*, *them*, etc.), or they find other words which mean the same thing (synonyms). For example:

a *... we can also take steps to keep our brains **healthy**? Experts recommend the following tips to keep your brain in good shape.*

b *Of course, the brain is a very **delicate** organ. It is easily damaged ...*

Which words or phrases mean **healthy** and **delicate**?

5 **Read Study Skill** Read paragraphs 1 and 2 of the article again. Look at the notes. Read the rest of the article, and complete the notes. Follow the order of the text. Use these headings:

- Socially active
- Brain-healthy diet
- Physical activity

STUDY SKILL Making notes (3)

One way of making notes is by making a list of points. Use bullets (•), dashes (–), or numbering (*1, 2, 3*, etc.) to group your notes.

Organizing notes in this way makes them easy to read and remember.

6 Answer the questions. Use your notes from exercise 5. Do not look at the article.

1 How can we stay mentally active? Give two examples.
2 How can we meet different people? Give two suggestions.
3 How is exercise good for the brain?
4 What kind of food is bad for the brain?
5 What food is good for the brain? Give examples.

Notes

- **How to keep body healthy**
  – a good diet
  – exercise, sleep
  – avoid smoking

  But we can also keep brains healthy. How?

- **Mentally active**
  Exercises for the brain, e.g:
  – quizzes
  – puzzles
  – maths problems

  Keep nerve cells sharp (creates new cells?)

- _____
  – _____
  – _____

- _____
  – _____
  – _____

- _____
  – _____
  – _____

Brain Quiz

1 How much does the human brain weigh?

   a less than 2 kilos   **c** 3–4 kilos

   b 2–3 kilos   **d** more than 4 kilos

2 Which has the heaviest brain?

   a a human   **c** a dolphin

   b an elephant   **d** a cow

3 How many neurons (nerve cells) are there in the brain?

   a 1 million   **c** 1 billion

   b 100 million   **d** 100 billion

4 The brain is one part of the central nervous system. What is the other part called?

   a the skin   **c** the lungs

   b the heart   **d** the spine

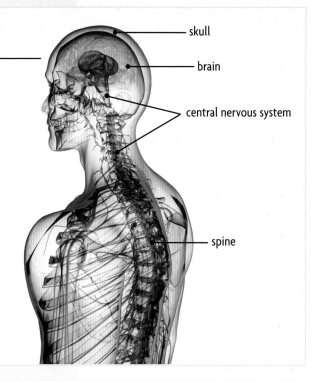

skull

brain

central nervous system

spine

HOW TO KEEP YOUR BRAIN HEALTHY

1 Most people know how to keep their bodies healthy. They know they should eat a good diet and try to get plenty of exercise and sleep. They should also avoid smoking, drinking, etc. However, do you know that we can also take steps to keep our brains healthy? Experts recommend the following tips to keep your brain in good shape.

2 _____. We <u>exercise</u> our bodies by walking, swimming, or going to the gym, but we can also do workouts for our brains. For example, we can try quizzes and word puzzles, or solve mathematical problems. This will keep the nerve cells sharp. It may also help to create new cells.

3 _____. This means that we should <u>socialize</u> by joining clubs and social groups. We can also mix with other people by travelling to other countries, or learning new skills. For example, we can do courses to learn skiing, dancing, or a new language.

4 _____. We know that exercise is <u>beneficial</u> for the body. However, it is also good for the brain. It keeps a good flow of blood to the brain, and encourages new cells. Of course, the brain is a very delicate organ. It is easily damaged, so people who like dangerous activities should be very careful. Rock climbers, cyclists, and cricket players should all protect their heads.

5 _____. This means we should <u>avoid</u> fatty foods. We should also stay away from food that is high in cholesterol. Instead, we should eat <u>nutritious</u> foods such as green vegetables, fruit, fish, and nuts. Foods which are good for you will protect the brain from disease. Certain foods, however, may actually <u>improve brainpower</u>. Research suggests that the nutrient 'choline', which is found in foods such as liver, eggs, and red meat, helps the brain work better.

Brain facts

- The human brain is part of the central nervous system, which also includes the spine.
- It consists of 100 billion neurons, or nerve cells, that send information to each other.
- The brain has many functions, such as memory, learning, and emotion.
- The skull, which is made of bone, protects the brain.
- The average human brain weighs 1300g–1400g This compares to 7500g for the brain of an elephant, 420g for a chimpanzee, 500g for a cow, 840g for a dolphin, and 30g for a cat.
- The human brain is about 2% of the average body weight.

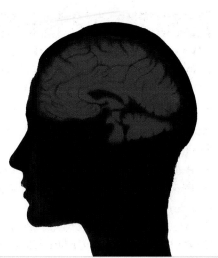

WRITING Notes and summaries

1 **Read Study Skill** Match a common mistake in the Study Skill box to the mistakes in sentences 1–6.

  1 My brother studying mathematics at the University of Milan.

  2 Bill Gates begins programming computers when he was 13 years old.

  3 Atilla is the student at Bilkent University, Ankara.

  4 How we can measure hurricanes?

  5 We know that exercise are good for the body.

  6 I have a lecture in Tuesday at 10 o'clock.

2 Look at a student's essay about Albert Einstein. Correct six more mistakes in the paragraph (see a–f in the Study Skill box).

STUDY SKILL Common mistakes

Language learners often repeat the same mistakes. For example, they make mistakes with:
a prepositions
b articles (*the, a, an*)
c missing words
d word order
e verb tenses
f subject/verb agreement

Know your strong and weak points, and always check your writing. Check the grammar, spelling, punctuation, and capital letters.

Albert Einstein was born in 1879 ~~at~~ *in* Germany. His family moved to Italy in 1894 and later he <u>lives</u> in Switzerland. He became a teacher of mathematics and physics in <u>the</u> secondary school and later he became a university lecturer. He was world famous for his research. He <u>were</u> probably most famous for the Theory of Relativity, <u>which in 1915 he discovered</u>. <u>On</u> 1921 he received the Nobel Prize. This award was for his research in physics and mathematics. Einstein ⋏ the greatest scientist of the 20th century. He died in 1955.

3 Think about your own writing. What is good about it? What mistakes do you make most? Discuss with a partner.

4 Read the article about sleep and complete the notes.

The importance of sleep

Why do we need to sleep? Sleep is very important for the brain. While we are asleep, the brain repairs itself. It also stores information that it learned during the day. If we do not get enough sleep, the brain cannot do these things. We become tired and we cannot remember things so well. Our body's 'immune system', which is its self-defence system, becomes weaker, so we are more likely to get ill.

What stops us sleeping? Most people find sleep difficult because they are not relaxed. They do not exercise enough during the day, and in the evening they are still thinking about their work or studies. In addition, they make phone calls or look at email messages until late at night. They also have too many drinks which contain caffeine, such as coffee, and eat dinner just before they go to bed. All of this is bad for sleeping.

What can we do? Of course, it is important to be relaxed. However, there are other things we can do to help us get a good night's sleep. First of all, we should make sure that the bed is comfortable, with a good mattress and pillows. The bedroom should be dark and quiet, so that we are not disturbed by light or noise. We should also have the same routine every evening before we go to bed. For example, we should read a book, have a hot bath, or listen to relaxing music. Finally, we should try to go to bed at the same time every night. In this way, we will start to sleep better and feel more active the next day.

1 **Importance of sleep.**
- during sleep: brain repairs itself
  stores _____
- no sleep: tired; cannot remember;
  may become _____

2 **What stops sleep?**
- not relaxed
- thinking about _____
- late at night: _____/emails
  _____/dinner

3 **What can we do to sleep well?**
- a comfortable bed
- a dark, quiet _____
- every night – same _____
  (book, _____, _____, etc.)

5 [Read Study Skill] Use the notes about sleep from exercise 4 and the prompts below to complete the summary.

Summary

During sleep the brain repairs itself and stores information. If we do not sleep, then we...

People sleep badly when they are not relaxed. They are thinking ... . Late at night they ...

To sleep well, we need ...

Writing a summary

6 Look at your notes about the brain from exercise 5 on page 52. Use the notes to write a summary of the article. Make sure you check your writing.

RESEARCH Books

1 **Read Study Skill** Look at the parts of a text book a–e. Label them.

2 Answer the questions.

1 What is the title of the book?
2 Who is the author?
3 When was the book first published?
4 Is this the author's only book?
5 Where can you find an alphabetical list of topics?
6 On which page can you find information on blood pressure?
7 Which chapter tells you about eating well?
8 Who is the book for – students, or scientists? Why do you think so?

3 Find a book that you want to read. Answer the questions.

1 What is the title of the book?
2 Who is the author?
3 When was the book first published?
4 Why do you want to read this book?
5 Will you read all of the book or just some parts?

4 Tell another student about the book and why you want to read it.

STUDY SKILL Reliable sources (2)

Before you read a book, have a look at it. Will it be useful? Use all of the information to help you decide. For example, you can use:

- the title page
- the contents page
- the back cover
- the printing history
- the index

b

c

a

Complete
BIOLOGY
W R Pickering

d

Complete Biology provides all the content needed for GCSE and IGCSE syllabuses. It is also an excellent text for Double Award Science candidates who may go on to take Biology at advanced level.

Although thoroughly addressing some of the harder concepts at this level, the author has achieved a high degree of clarity in presenting ideas, using many original diagrams and straightforward explanations.

There are questions on each double-page spread for students to check their understanding, and learning objectives to enable users to identify relevant pages at a glance.

In the same series:

Complete Chemistry
by RoseMarie Gallagher and Paul Ingram

Complete Physics
by Stephen Pople

By the same author:

Oxford Revision Guides

GCSE Biology

A level Biology

A level Human Biology

OXFORD
UNIVERSITY PRESS

www.OxfordSecondary.co.uk

ISBN 0-19-914739-6

9 780199 147397

e

REVIEW

1 Label the parts of the human body. Some words are from Unit 9. Use your dictionary to help.

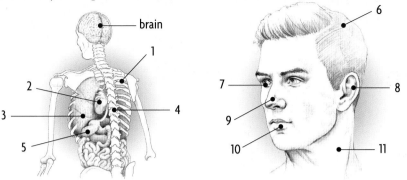

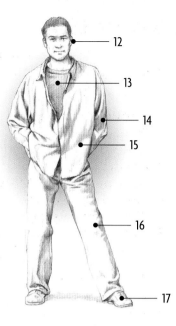

2 Read the paragraph about Albert Einstein's brain. There are twelve mistakes. What kind of mistakes are they? Choose from the box.

punctuation	capital letters	word order	missing words	spelling
preposition	incorrect article	verb tense	subject/verb agreement	

Einstein's brain

What <u>know we do</u> about Einstein's brain ⋀ We know quite a lot. Because Albert Einstein was <u>the</u> great mathematician and <u>sceintist</u>, other scientists wanted to study his brain. He agreed that after his death they could use ⋀ brain for research. When <u>einstein</u> died <u>at</u> 1955 at the age of 76, scientists began to <u>studying</u> his brain. They found that his brain <u>were</u> the same as other brains. In fact, its weight was less than the average male brain. However ⋀ one thing was unusual. His brain was 15% wider ⋀ normal. <u>this</u> area was the part of the brain responsible for mathematical thinking.

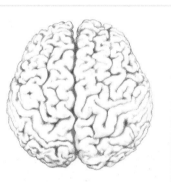

3 Work in small groups to correct the mistakes.

4 Match words 1–6 with the words and phrases a–f.

1	☐ beneficial	a	do work outs
2	☐ avoid	b	easily damaged
3	☐ healthy	c	good for
4	☐ exercise	d	mix with other people
5	☐ socialize	e	stay away from
6	☐ delicate	f	in good shape

5 Complete the sentences with words 1–6 from exercise 4.

1 It is important to _____ our brains by doing puzzles and quizzes.
2 Fresh fruit and vegetables are _____ for the body and the brain.
3 You must protect the brain when you do dangerous sports. It is a very _____ organ.
4 If you want to stay healthy, _____ foods that are full of fat and sugar.
5 Scientists say it is important to _____ with people. It helps the brain stay active.
6 When you are studying, keep your body and brain _____. Do exercise, eat good food, and sleep.

6 Choose a topic on health, for example, *Keeping your brain healthy, The importance of sleep,* etc. Think of tips on what people should and shouldn't do. Make a poster to display in class.

10 Staying alive

READING SKILLS Using what you know • Using reference to understand a text • Focusing on statistics
WRITING SKILLS Linking ideas (8), (9), and (10) • Words and phrases (3) • Writing about statistics
VOCABULARY DEVELOPMENT Words or figures? • Learning a word – synonyms and antonyms

READING Dangerous diseases of our time

1 What are the most serious diseases in the world?

Heart disease, …

2 What are *developed* and *developing* countries? Give two examples of each.

3 [Read Study Skill] Work in pairs. How much do you know about diabetes? Discuss the questions.

1 What is diabetes?
2 Which countries have the highest rate of diabetes – developed, or developing?
3 Will the number of people with diabetes rise (↑) or fall (↓) in the future?
4 What causes diabetes?
5 How can we avoid getting it?

4 Skim the article *Diabetes: a growing world danger* on page 59. Which paragraph tells us… ?

a ☐ how to avoid diabetes
b ☐ unhealthy lifestyles in rich countries
c ☐ diabetes death rates
d ☐ why people live longer in rich countries
e ☐ what will happen in the future

5 Read the article. Check your answers to exercise 3 above.

6 [Read Study Skill] Look at the underlined pronouns in the article. What do they refer to?

Pronoun	refers to
They – who? (paragraph 1)	*the inhabitants*
it – what? (paragraph 1)	
They – who? (paragraph 2)	
which – what? (paragraph 2)	
which – what? (paragraph 3)	
Here – where? (paragraph 4)	
it – what? (paragraph 5)	

7 [Read Study Skill] Scan the article and complete the three tables with the correct figures.

8 Find statistics about another country (e.g. your country) for life expectancy and diabetes. Make a note of the source you use.

STUDY SKILL Using what you know

Before you read about a topic, for example *diabetes*, ask yourself: What do I already know about this topic?

You may know more than you think. Your knowledge will help you read and understand the text.

STUDY SKILL Using reference to understand a text

When writers refer back to something they said earlier, they may use:

- **personal pronouns**, such as *he, him, it, they, them*
- **possessive adjectives and pronouns**, such as *his, its, their, theirs* (see Unit 7 p43)
- **relative pronouns**, such as *which* and *where* (see Unit 8 p49).

Writers can also use **adverbs** such as *here* and *there* to refer back to a place. For example:
Japan is a wealthy country. **Here** *the standard of living is very high.*
Botswana is a poor country. Life expectancy is very low **there***.*

It is important for a reader to understand reference. Reference helps the reader understand the text.

STUDY SKILL Focusing on statistics

Remember – visuals in a text are an important part of that text. Visuals such as tables, charts, and graphs organize the statistics for the reader. They make the statistics easier to understand. Read the text carefully, but also study the visuals to get the complete idea.

Diabetes: a growing world danger

1 As a country develops, the inhabitants usually become wealthier – and healthier. <u>They</u> have better health care, drink cleaner water, and eat better food. Both men and women can expect to live longer. For example, **TABLE A** shows that in Japan the average life expectancy at birth for men is 77.6 years, and for women is 84.6 years. On the other hand, in a developing country like Botswana, <u>it</u> is just 37 for men and 36 for women.

2 However, in developed countries, lifestyle and diet are changing. People have busier lives. <u>They</u> are working longer hours, so they are more likely to suffer from stress. They do not have time to prepare proper meals. They eat processed or fast food instead, <u>which</u> contains a higher proportion of fat, salt, and sugar. They do not walk so much, and some do not do any physical activity at all. As a result, the percentage of the population with heart disease or cancer is increasing.

3 Another disease that has become more common in richer countries is diabetes. This is a disease in which the body cannot control the level of sugar in the blood. Diabetes is caused by poor diet and a lack of exercise. We can see from **TABLE B** that Germany, <u>which</u> is a developed country, has 183.7 deaths per million people. On the other hand, in Peru, a developing country, the death rate is just 61.3 per million people. The rate in Germany is more than three times the rate in Peru.

4 We can also see from the statistics in **TABLE C** that the number of people with diabetes is rising. In the year 2003, according to the World Health Organization (the WHO), 194 million adults had diabetes – about 5.1% of the population. By 2030, the WHO say this figure will be about 366 million (6.3%). The Middle East, they say, will see the biggest increase. <u>Here</u> the total will go up from 15.2 million people to 42.6 million by 2030.

5 It is possible to control diabetes with drugs, but there is no cure. There are things, however, that people, especially young people, can do to avoid <u>it</u>. If they are overweight, they should try to lose weight. They should also watch what they eat and try to avoid foods high in fats and sugars. People should exercise regularly by jogging, swimming, or doing aerobics. In addition, they should walk or cycle more instead of travelling by car or bus. If people change to this healthier lifestyle, we may be able to stop the rise in diabetes in the future.

TABLE A   LIFE EXPECTANCY

	men	**women**
Japan	_____	_____
Botswana	_____	_____

TABLE B   DEATH RATES FOR DIABETES

	deaths per million population
Germany	_____
Peru	_____

TABLE C   DIABETES WORLDWIDE

	2003	**2030**
People (aged 20–79) with diabetes	_____	_____
Percentage (%) of population	_____	_____

WRITING Describing statistics

1 `Read Study Skill` Complete the sentences with a contrast clause.

STUDY SKILL Linking ideas (8)

On the other hand

We use linking words such as *however* and *but* to contrast ideas (see Study Skill p29). We can also use *on the other hand*.

In Europe there were no deaths from Malaria in 2002. **On the other hand**, *in Africa, there were 1,136,00.*

Find two examples of *on the other hand* in the article on diabetes. Underline them, and circle the commas.

---

1 Germany is quite a rich country. On the other hand, Botswana …
2 The courses at Central College are very expensive. On the other hand, …
3 Mobile phones are very useful. On the other hand, …
4 Running is good exercise and helps you to lose weight. On the other hand, …

2 `Read Study Skill` Complete the sentences with a result clause.

STUDY SKILL Linking ideas (9)

As a result

We use *so* to link ideas in a sentence and to show a result (see Study Skill p24).
A similar linking phrase is *as a result*.

The world is not doing enough to stop the spread of malaria. **As a result**, *there are more than 1.2 million deaths from malaria every year.*

Find an example of *as a result* in paragraph 2 of the article on diabetes. Underline it, and circle the comma.

---

1 People in some European countries have very small families. As a result, …
2 These days, most people know that smoking causes cancer. As a result, …
3 My cousin speaks five languages fluently. As a result, …
4 Canada has beautiful mountains and lakes. As a result, …

3 `Read Study Skill` Match sentences 1–6 with a–f. Rewrite them using *also*.

STUDY SKILL Linking ideas (10)

Also

We use linking words and phrases such as *in addition* and *and* to introduce a similar idea or extra information (see Study Skill p42).
A similar linking word is *also*. It usually comes before the main verb, or after the verb *to be*.

The lowest number of deaths from malaria was in Europe. The Americas and the Western Pacific **also** *had a small number of deaths.*

The number of deaths in Europe is low. It is **also** *low in the Americas and the Western Pacific.*

Find two examples of *also* in the article on diabetes, and underline them.

---

1 ☐ Fast food contains a lot of fat.	a It can be a very difficult subject for students.
2 ☐ Diabetes is very common in European countries.	b It has a lot of salt and sugar.
3 ☐ Sam runs for five kilometres every morning before college.	c He goes to the gym twice a week.
4 ☐ A degree in medicine is expensive because it takes many years.	d His level of cholesterol is very high.
5 ☐ Elena would like to have her own company one day.	e Her sister wants to go into business.
6 ☐ Henry has high blood pressure.	f There are many people with diabetes in Africa and the Middle East.

4 Look at the table on deaths from malaria in six different regions of the world. Answer the questions.

DEATHS FROM MALARIA – 2002		
region	**number of deaths**	**% of global total**
Africa	1,136,000	89.3
South-East Asia	65,000	5.1
Americas	1,000	less than 1
Western Pacific	11,000	less than 1
Eastern Mediterranean	59,000	4.6
Europe	0	0
World	1,272,000	100

1 Which region has the highest number of deaths from malaria?
2 Which region has the lowest number of deaths?
3 How many people in the Eastern Mediterranean died from malaria in 2002?
4 What percentage of the world total were Eastern Mediterranean?
5 What was the total number of deaths from malaria in the world in 2002?

5 **Read Study Skill** Study the table about deaths from malaria again. Complete the paragraph about the table with the words and numbers.

89.3%	was	65,000	one million	number
see	no	4.6%	shows	5.1%

The table ¹_____ the number of deaths from malaria in 2002 in six different regions of the world. We can ²_____ that most deaths from malaria occurred in Africa. More than ³_____ people died in 2002, which was ⁴_____ of all the deaths in the world. The second largest ⁵_____ of deaths was in South-East Asia. About ⁶_____ people died, which was ⁷_____ of the total. The third largest number is in the Eastern Mediterranean region. The number of deaths ⁸_____ 59,000, which was ⁹_____. In Europe, however, there were ¹⁰_____ deaths during this year.

Writing about statistics

6 Look at the table on life expectancy in different regions of the world. Describe the statistics for males, females, or both. Use the language in the Study Skill box. For example:

The table shows life expectancy in …
In Africa the life expectancy for males was 49 in 2002.
By 2025 this figure will increase to …

LIFE EXPECTANCY				
region	**2002**		**2025**	
	males	**females**	**males**	**females**
Africa	49	51	53	57
Near East	67	71	72	77
Asia	65	68	71	75
Latin America and the Caribbean	68	74	73	79
Europe	69	76	73	81
North America	74	78	78	84

VOCABULARY DEVELOPMENT Numbers in texts

1 Underline the numbers in the sentences. `Read Study Skill`

1 A hundred and fifty-three workers were injured in the fire.
2 The fire injured 153 workers.
3 The politicians visited six cities in a week.
4 The Taj Mahal is more than 450 years old.
5 Rashid was first in the boxing competition.
6 The meeting is on the 3rd October 2006.
7 The price of cars has increased by 12% this year.
8 The room was 6.5 m wide.

2 Correct the sentences using the rules in the Study Skill box.

1 More than two thousand, five hundred and sixty people live in my village.
2 There were 4 cars outside my house.
3 245 people died in the plane crash.
4 China has the 2nd largest number of people with diabetes.
5 Salaries will go up by fifteen point five per cent next month.

Using antonyms and synonyms

3 `Read Study Skill` Use a dictionary to find the antonyms of the words in bold. Use the antonyms to complete the sentences.

1 This water is **dirty**. There is some _____ water in the bottle.
2 In general, the rate of cancer will **increase** in the future, but in some countries it will _____.
3 This food contains a **high** proportion of fat. Try to eat _____ fat food such as skimmed milk.
4 The plane will **depart** at 10.55 and _____ in London at 16.30.
5 Physics is usually a **difficult** subject, but yesterday's physics exam was very _____.
6 The first conference at the university was a great **success**. More than 100 people came. However, the second conference was a _____. Only 12 people came.

4 Replace the words in bold with a synonym.

1 Martha is a fast reader. She is also very **fast** at mathematical calculations.
2 I am quite nervous about starting the new job. I am **nervous** about meeting the boss.
3 I am not interested in the subject. It is very dull. The lecturer is **dull** too.
4 The ideal time for picnics is in the spring. The **ideal** place is near a river or in a park.
5 I will ring the bank on Saturday. I will also **ring** the airline to book the tickets.
6 The company would like to purchase a new photocopier. We also need to **purchase** some desks and office chairs.

REVIEW

1 Complete the table with the correct noun or verb. Use your dictionary to help.

2 Complete the sentences with nouns from the table.

1 The _____ expectancy in Botswana in Africa is very low.
2 The _____ rate from diabetes is increasing in developed countries.
3 The population of many developing countries is increasing. Pakistan has the highest _____ rate in the world.
4 Last year there were 15,000 students in the university and now there are 20,000. This is an _____ of 33%.
5 The price of oil went down last month. There was a _____ of $5.3 per barrel.

verb	noun
to be born	
	a life
to die	
	an increase
to rise	
to decrease	
	a fall

3 Use negative prefixes to make the antonyms of the words.

1 healthy _____
2 expensive _____
3 personal _____
4 approve _____

5 legal _____
6 interesting _____
7 possible _____
8 organized _____

Spelling (4) -ing forms

4 Read the rules. Copy and complete the table with verbs from the unit. Add other verbs that you know.

verb + -ing	~e + -ing	double consonant + -ing

RULES Spelling -ing forms

- most verbs: + -ing: develop/developing
- verbs ending in -e: ~e + -ing: rise/rising
- a one-syllable verb ending in vowel + consonant: double the consonant + -ing: jog/jogging

5 Read the paragraph about birth and death rates worldwide. Complete the table with details of *who, what,* or *where* the pronouns refer to.

1 The bar chart shows the birth and death rates in the world by region. It indicates that the
2 region with the highest birth rate is Africa. Here the rate is over 35 births per 1000 people. It is
3 much higher than the death rate, which is under 15 deaths per thousand. The region with the
4 lowest birth rate is Europe, where the rate is just over 10 births per 1000 people. However, the
5 chart also shows that the death rate here is higher than the birth rate. It is approximately 12
6 deaths per 1000. These figures mean that the population of Europe is declining slowly. The
7 countries of Asia have birth rates of just over 20 births per 1000. They have rates that are about
8 the same as the world average. This is the same as the rate in Latin America.

pronoun	refers to
It (line 1)	the bar chart
Here (line 2)	
It (line 2)	
which (line 3)	
where (line 4)	
here (line 5)	
It (line 5)	
They (line 7)	

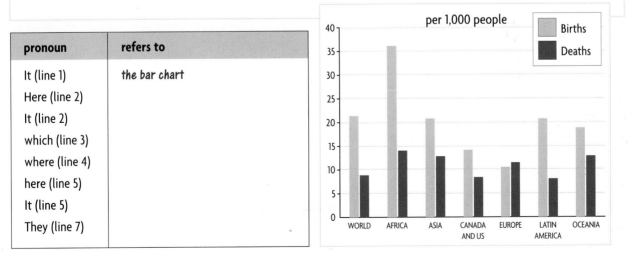

WORDLIST

Here is a list of most of the new words in the units of *New Headway Academic Skills* Level 1 Student's Book.

adj = adjective
adv = adverb
conj = conjunction
n = noun
pl = plural
prep = preposition
pron = pronoun
US = American English
v = verb

Unit 1

accountant *n* /əˈkaʊntənt/
adjective *n* /ˈædʒɪktɪv/
adverb *n* /ˈædvɜːb/
all *adv* /ɔːl/
always *adv* /ˈɔːlweɪz/
American *adj* /əˈmerɪkən/
anywhere *adv* /ˈeniweə(r)/
apartment *n* /əˈpɑːtmənt/
Arabic *n* /ˈærəbɪk/
article *n* /ˈɑːtɪkl/
assistant *n* /əˈsɪstənt/
as well as /əz ˈwel əz/
at the start /ət ðə ˈstɑːt/
aunt *n* /ɑːnt/

Bahrain *n* /bɑːˈreɪn/
bank *n* /bæŋk/
big *adj* /bɪg/
brain *n* /breɪn/
Brazil *n* /brəˈzɪl/
break down *v* /ˌbreɪk ˈdaʊn/
British *adj* /ˈbrɪtɪʃ/
brother *n* /ˈbrʌðə(r)/
build *v* /bɪld/
builder *n* /ˈbɪldə(r)/
bungalow *n* /ˈbʌŋgələʊ/
business *n* /ˈbɪznəs/
buy *v* /baɪ/

café *n* /ˈkæfeɪ/
campus *n* /ˈkæmpəs/
capital (city) *n* /ˌkæpɪtl (ˈsɪti)/
carefully *adv* /ˈkeəfəli/
carry *v* /ˈkæri/
chapter *n* /ˈtʃæptə(r)/
check *v* /tʃek/
China *n* /ˈtʃaɪnə/
Chinese *adj, n* /tʃaɪˈniːz/
choose *v* /tʃuːz/
comfortable *adj* /ˈkʌmftəbl/
computers *n pl* /kəmˈpjuːtəz/
computer games *n pl*
    /kəmˈpjuːtə ˌgeɪmz/
computer programming *n*
    /kəmˈpjuːtə ˈprəʊgræmɪŋ/
computing *n* /kəmˈpjuːtɪŋ/

continue *v* /kənˈtɪnjuː/
correct *adj* /kəˈrekt/
course *n* /kɔːs/
cousin *n* /ˈkʌzn/

desk *n* /desk/
different *adj* /ˈdɪfrənt/
difficult *adj* /ˈdɪfɪkəlt/
doctor *n* /ˈdɒktə(r)/

easy *adj* /ˈiːzi/
equation *n* /ɪˈkweɪʒn/
evenings *n pl* /ˈiːvnɪŋz/
every *adj* /ˈevri/
everything *pron* /ˈevriθɪŋ/
excellent *adj* /ˈeksələnt/

faculty *n* /ˈfækəlti/
Farsi *n* /ˈfɑːsi/
father *n* /ˈfɑːðə(r)/
a few /ə ˈfjuː/
finally *adv* /ˈfaɪnəli/
find *v* /faɪnd/
flat *n* /flæt/
floor *n* /flɔː(r)/
free time *n* /ˌfriː ˈtaɪm/
French *n* /frentʃ/
future *n* /ˈfjuːtʃə(r)/

general idea *n* /ˌdʒenrəl aɪˈdɪə/
German *n* /ˈdʒɜːmən/
Germany *n* /ˈdʒɜːməni/
graduate *n* /ˈgrædjuːət/
grandmother *n* /ˈgrænmʌðə(r)/

heading *n pl* /ˈhedɪŋ/
history *n* /ˈhɪstri/
Holland *n* /ˈhɒlənd/
hope *v* /həʊp/
hostel *n* /ˈhɒstl/
hotel *n* /həʊˈtel/
house *n* /haʊs/

India *n* /ˈɪndiə/
information *n* /ˌɪnfəˈmeɪʃn/
institute *n* /ˈɪnstɪtjuːt/
interesting *adj* /ˈɪntrəstɪŋ/
Internet café *n* /ˈɪntənet ˌkæfeɪ/
in this case /ˌɪn ˈðɪs ˌkeɪs/
island *n* /ˈaɪlənd/

journey *n* /ˈdʒɜːni/

kitchen *n* /ˈkɪtʃɪn/
knowledge *n* /ˈnɒlɪdʒ/

language *n* /ˈlæŋgwɪdʒ/
large *adj* /lɑːdʒ/
late *adj* /leɪt/
learn by heart *v* /ˌlɜːn baɪ ˈhɑːt/
library *n* /ˈlaɪbrəri/
link *v* /lɪŋk/
look through *v* /ˈlʊk ˌθruː/
lorry *n* /ˈlɒri/

magazine *n* /ˌmægəˈziːn/
Malay *n* /məˈleɪ/
married *adj* /ˈmærɪd/
mathematical *adj* /ˌmæθəˈmætɪkl/
mathematics *n* /ˌmæθəˈmætɪks/
meaning *n* /ˈmiːnɪŋ/

message *n* /ˈmesɪdʒ/
Middle East *n* /ˌmɪdl ˈiːst/
mother *n* /ˈmʌðə(r)/

need *v* /niːd/
never *adv* /ˈnevə(r)/
newspaper *n* /ˈnjuːspeɪpə(r)/
notebook *n* /ˈnəʊtbʊk/
noun *n* /naʊn/
novel *n* /ˈnɒvl/

one day /ˌwʌn ˈdeɪ/
only *adv* /ˈəʊnli/
opposite *n* /ˈɒpəzɪt/
organization *n* /ˌɔːgənaɪˈzeɪʃn/
other *adj* /ˈʌðə(r)/

palace *n* /ˈpæləs/
paragraph *n* /ˈpærəgrɑːf/
parents *n pl* /ˈpeərənts/
park *n* /pɑːk/
part of speech *n* /ˌpɑːt əv ˈspiːtʃ/
perhaps *adv* /pəˈhæps/
PhD *n* /ˌpiː eɪtʃ ˈdiː/
physics *n* /ˈfɪzɪks/
pianist *n* /ˈpɪənɪst/
pilot *n* /ˈpaɪlət/
place *n* /pleɪs/
plural *n* /ˈplʊərəl/
poem *n* /ˈpəʊɪm/
poetry *n* /ˈpəʊətri/
Portugal *n* /ˈpɔːtʃʊgl/
preposition *n* /ˌprepəˈzɪʃn/
professor *n* /prəˈfesə(r)/
pronounce *v* /prəˈnaʊns/
pronunciation *n* /prəˌnʌnsiˈeɪʃn/

quick *adj* /kwɪk/
quickly *adv* /ˈkwɪkli/
quite *adv* /kwaɪt/
quiz *n* /kwɪz/

reader *n* /ˈriːdə(r)/
receptionist *n* /rɪˈsepʃənɪst/
remember *v* /rɪˈmembə(r)/
report *n* /rɪˈpɔːt/
research *n* /rɪˈsɜːtʃ, ˈriːsɜːtʃ/
restaurant *n* /ˈrestrɒnt/
return *v* /rɪˈtɜːn/
right *adj* /raɪt/
Russian *n* /ˈrʌʃn/

scanning *n* /ˈskænɪŋ/
science *n* /ˈsaɪəns/
Singapore *n* /ˌsɪŋəˈpɔː(r)/
single *adj* /ˈsɪŋgl/
sister *n* /ˈsɪstə(r)/
slowly *adv* /ˈsləʊli/
skimming *n* /ˈskɪmɪŋ/
small *adj* /smɔːl/
sofa *n* /ˈsəʊfə/
sometimes *adv* /ˈsʌmtaɪmz/
south *n* /saʊθ/
speeds *n pl* /spiːdz/
student *n* /ˈstjuːdənt/
study reading *n* /ˈstʌdi ˌriːdɪŋ/
suburb *n* /ˈsʌbɜːb/
summer *n* /ˈsʌmə(r)/

teach *v* /tiːtʃ/
technical *adj* /ˈteknɪkl/
telephone directory *n*
    /ˈtelɪfəʊn dəˌrektəri/
telephone number *n*
    /ˈtelɪfəʊn ˌnʌmbə(r)/
textbook *n* /ˈtekstbʊk/
timetable *n* /ˈtaɪmteɪbl/
topic *n* /ˈtɒpɪk/
town *n* /taʊn/
translator *n* /trænsˈleɪtə(r)/
Turkey *n* /ˈtɜːki/
type *n* /taɪp/

uncle *n* /ˈʌŋkl/
university *n* /ˌjuːnɪˈvɜːsəti/
USA *n* /ˌjuː es ˈeɪ/
useful *adj* /ˈjuːsfl/
usually *adv* /ˈjuːʒʊəli/

verb *n* /vɜːb/
villa *n* /ˈvɪlə/

way *n* /weɪ/
well *adv* /wel/

Unit 2

academic *adj* /ˌækəˈdemɪk/
accident *n* /ˈæksɪdənt/
according to *prep* /əˈkɔːdɪŋ tə/
actor *n* /ˈæktə(r)/
airport *n* /ˈeəpɔːt/
assistant manager *n*
   /əˌsɪstənt ˈmænɪdʒə(r)/
attend *v* /əˈtend/
author *n* /ˈɔːθə(r)/

block style *n* /ˈblɒk ˌstaɪl/
breakfast *n* /ˈbrekfəst/
breaks *n pl* /breɪks/
burning *adj* /ˈbɜːnɪŋ/
business *n* /ˈbɪznəs/
business studies *n pl*
   /ˈbɪznəs ˌstʌdiz/
busy *adj* /ˈbɪzi/

canteen *n* /kænˈtiːn/
capital letters *n pl* /ˌkæpɪtl ˈletəz/
catch *v* /kætʃ/
change *v* /tʃeɪndʒ/
chemical engineering *n*
   /ˌkemɪkl ˌendʒɪˈnɪərɪŋ/
clearly *adv* /ˈklɪəli/
coffee *n* /ˈkɒfi/
coffee shop *n* /ˈkɒfi ˌʃɒp/
collect *v* /kəˈlekt/
college *n* /ˈkɒlɪdʒ/
common *adj* /ˈkɒmən/
company *n* /ˈkʌmpəni/
computer *n* /kəmˈpjuːtə(r)/
computer virus *n*
   /kəmˈpjuːtə ˌvaɪrəs/
customers *n pl* /ˈkʌstəməz/

dangerous *adj* /ˈdeɪndʒərəs/
direction *n* /dəˈrekʃn, dɪ-, daɪ-/
drive *v* /draɪv/

early *adj* /ˈɜːli/
email *n* /ˈiːmeɪl/
essay *n* /ˈeseɪ/
exams *n pl* /ɪgˈzæmz/

face *v* /feɪs/
fill in *v* /ˌfɪl ˈɪn/
finally *adv* /ˈfaɪnəli/
firstly *adv* /ˈfɜːstli/
fit *adj* /fɪt/
fireman *n* /ˈfaɪəmən/
fires *n pl* /ˈfaɪəz/
florist *n* /ˈflɒrɪst/
flowers *n pl* /ˈflaʊəz/
following *adj* /ˈfɒləʊɪŋ/
form *n, v* /fɔːm/

guests *n pl* /gests/

handwriting *n* /ˈhændraɪtɪŋ/
head (of a company) *n* /hed/
healthy *adj* /ˈhelθi/
however *conj* /haʊˈevə(r)/
husband *n* /ˈhʌzbənd/

important *adj* /ɪmˈpɔːtənt/
indented *adj* /ɪnˈdentɪd/
in order to /ɪn ˈɔːdə tə/
Internet *n* /ˈɪntənet/
interpreter *n* /ɪnˈtɜːprɪtə(r)/
journalist *n* /ˈdʒɜːnəlɪst/

keep fit *v* /ˌkiːp ˈfɪt/
leave *v* /liːv/
left-hand *adj* /ˈleft ˌhænd/
link *v* /lɪŋk/
long *adj* /lɒŋ/
lose weight *v* /ˌluːz ˈweɪt/
lucky *adj* /ˈlʌki/
lunch *n* /lʌntʃ/

main *adj* /meɪn/
manager *n* /ˈmænɪdʒə(r)/
managing director *n* /ˌmænɪdʒɪŋ
   dəˈrektə(r), dɪ-, daɪ/
mark *v* /mɑːk/
market *n* /ˈmɑːkɪt/
Master's degree *n*
   /ˈmɑːstəz dɪˌgriː/
MD *n* /ˌem ˈdiː/
meeting *n* /ˈmiːtɪŋ/

next *adv* /nekst/
notes *n pl* /nəʊts/
nutritionist *n* /njuˈtrɪʃənɪst/

office *n* /ˈɒfɪs/
oil *n* /ɔɪl/
on the other hand
   /ˌɒn ði ˈʌðə ˌhænd/
overseas *adv* /ˌəʊvəˈsiːz/

pass *v* /pɑːs/
passengers *n pl* /ˈpæsɪndʒəz/
perfect *adj* /ˈpɜːfɪkt/
personal trainer *n*
   /ˌpɜːsənl ˈtreɪnə(r)/
pick-up truck *n* /ˈpɪk ʌp ˌtrʌk/
picnics *n pl* /ˈpɪknɪks/
plan *n* /plæn/
plants *n pl* /plɑːnts/
point *v* /pɔɪnt/
points *n pl* /pɔɪnts/
predict *v* /prɪˈdɪkt/
prepare *v* /prɪˈpeə(r)/
problems *n pl* /ˈprɒbləmz/
procedure *n* /prəˈsiːdʒə(r)/
put out *v* /ˌpʊt ˈaʊt/

quiet *adj* /ˈkwaɪət/

reasons *n pl* /ˈriːznz/
relatives *n pl* /ˈrelətɪvz/
relaxing *adj* /rɪˈlæksɪŋ/
revise *v* /rɪˈvaɪz/
routine *n* /ruːˈtiːn/
run (a company) *v* /rʌn/

salary *n* /ˈsæləri/
save *v* /seɪv/
scan *v* /skæn/
scientist *n* /ˈsaɪəntɪst/
search *n* /sɜːtʃ/
secondary school *n*
   /ˈsekəndri ˌskuːl/
semester *n* /səˈmestə(r)/
send *v* /send/
sequencing words *n pl*
   /ˈsiːkwənsɪŋ ˌwɜːdz/
shopkeeper *n* /ˈʃɒpkiːpə(r)/
show *v* /ʃəʊ/
snack bar *n* /ˈsnæk ˌbɑː(r)/
space *n* /speɪs/
spend *v* /spend/
staff *n* /stɑːf/
start up *v* /ˌstɑːt ˈʌp/

steps *n pl* /steps/
stress *n* /stres/
stressful *adj* /ˈstresfl/
studies *n pl* /ˈstʌdiz/
summary *n* /ˈsʌməri/
survey *n* /ˈsɜːveɪ/
syllabus *n* /ˈsɪləbəs/

taxi *n* /ˈtæksi/
taxi-driver *n* /ˈtæksi ˌdraɪvə(r)/
tea *n* /tiː/
telephone calls *n pl*
   /ˈtelɪfəʊn ˌkɔːlz/
tell *v* /tel/
toast *n* /təʊst/
too *adv* /tuː/
traffic *n* /ˈtræfɪk/
traffic jam *n* /ˈtræfɪk ˌdʒæm/
traffic lights *n pl* /ˈtræfɪk ˌlaɪts/
traffic warden *n* /ˈtræfɪk ˌwɔːdn/
train *v* /treɪn/

unhealthy *adj* /ʌnˈhelθi/

visit *v* /ˈvɪzɪt/

weather *n* /ˈweðə(r)/
weekend *n* /ˌwiːkˈend/
well-paid *adj* /ˌwel ˈpeɪd/
while *conj* /waɪl/
worry *n* /ˈwʌri/

Unit 3

Africa *n* /ˈæfrɪkə/
alone *adj* /əˈləʊn/
always *adv* /ˈɔːlweɪz/
and so on /ən ˈsəʊ ˌɒn/
animals *n pl* /ˈænɪmlz/
Antarctica *n* /ænˈtɑːktɪkə/
anti-clockwise *adv*
   /ˌænti ˈklɒkwaɪz/
apostrophes *n pl* /əˈpɒstrəfiz/
area *n* /ˈeəriə/
Atlantic (Ocean) *n*
   /ət̩ˌlæntɪk (ˈəʊʃn)/
Australia *n* /ɒˈstreɪliə/
autumn *n* /ˈɔːtəm/

beach *n* /biːtʃ/
Bhutan *n v* /buːˈtɑːn/
blue *adj* /bluː/

camels *n pl* /ˈkæmlz/
camping *n* /ˈkæmpɪŋ/
Caribbean Sea *n* /ˌkærəˌbiːən ˈsiː/
category *n* /ˈkætəgəri/
cause *v* /kɔːz/
centre *n* /ˈsentə(r)/
chat *v* /tʃæt/
cinema *n* /ˈsɪnəmə/
city *n* /ˈsɪti/
climate *n* /ˈklaɪmət/
clothes *n pl* /kləʊðz/
cloud *n* /klaʊd/
cloud over *v* /klaʊd ˈəʊvə(r)/
cloudy *adj* /ˈklaʊdi/
cold *adj* /kəʊld/
collect *v* /kəˈlekt/
consult *v* /kənˈsʌlt/
context *n* /ˈkɒntekst/
contractions *n pl* /kənˈtrækʃnz/
cook *v* /kʊk/
countryside *n* /ˈkʌntrisaɪd/
cover *v* /ˈkʌvə(r)/

dacha *n* /ˈdætʃə/
damage *n* /ˈdæmɪdʒ/
define *v* /dɪˈfaɪn/
definition *n* /ˌdefɪˈnɪʃn/
description *n* /dɪˈskrɪpʃn/
desert *n* /ˈdezət/
diagrams *n pl* /ˈdaɪəgræmz/
divide *v* /dɪˈvaɪd/
drawings *n pl* /ˈdrɔːɪŋz/
dry *adj* /draɪ/

Earth *n* /ɜːθ/
economic *adj* /ˌiːkəˈnɒmɪk, ˌekə-/
encyclopaedia *n* /ɪnˌsaɪkləˈpiːdiə/
entry *n* /ˈentri/
except for *prep* /ɪkˈsept fə(r)/
extract *n* /ˈekstrækt/
eye (of a hurricane) *n* /aɪ/

favourite *adj* /ˈfeɪvərɪt/
follow *v* /ˈfɒləʊ/
forest *n* /ˈfɒrɪst/
formal *adj* /ˈfɔːml/
formality *n* /fɔːˈmæləti/
fortunately *adv* /ˈfɔːtʃənətli/
foxes *n pl* /ˈfɒksɪz/
freezing cold *adj* /ˌfriːzɪŋ ˈkəʊld/
friends *n pl* /frendz/
fruit trees *n pl* /ˈfruːt ˌtriːz/

garage *n* /ˈgærɑːʒ, ˈgærɪdʒ/
garden *n* /ˈgɑːdn/
global *adj* /ˈgləʊbl/
go on *v* /ˌgəʊ ˈɒn/
grade *v* /greɪd/
grey *adj* /greɪ/
grow *v* /grəʊ/
guess *v* /ges/
Gulf of Mexico *n*
   /ˌgʌlf əv ˈmeksɪkəʊ/

habits *n pl* /ˈhæbɪts/
headings *n pl* /ˈhedɪŋz/
headlines *n pl* /ˈhedlaɪnz/
heavy *adj* /ˈhevi/
heat *n, v* /hiːt/
high *adj* /haɪ/
high point *n* /ˈhaɪ ˌpɔɪnt/
home *n* /həʊm/
hot *adj* /hɒt/
huge *adj* /hjuːdʒ/
hurricane *n* /ˈhʌrɪkən/

ice *n* /aɪs/
ice over *v* /ˌaɪs ˈəʊvə(r)/
icy *adj* /ˈaɪsi/
identify *v* /aɪˈdentɪfaɪ/
inches *n pl* /ˈɪntʃɪz/
insects *n pl* /ˈɪnsekts/
institute *n* /ˈɪnstɪtjuːt/
interview *v* /ˈɪntəvjuː/

Japan *n* /dʒəˈpæn/

kms *n pl* /ˌkeɪ ˈem, ˈkɪləmiːtəz,
   kɪˈlɒmɪtəz/

lake *n* /leɪk/
land *n* /lænd/
Law of Gravity *n*
   /ˌlɔːr əv ˈgrævəti/
lectures *n pl* /ˈlektʃəz/
life *n* /laɪf/
location *n* /ləʊˈkeɪʃn/
look up *v* /ˌlʊk ˈʌp/
love *v* /lʌv/

make *n* /meɪk/
meals *n pl* /miːlz/
measure *v* /ˈmeʒə(r)/
mm *n* /ˌem ˈem, ˈmɪlimiːtəz/
mobile phone *n* /ˌməʊbaɪl ˈfəʊn/
months *n pl* /mʌnθs/
mountains *n pl* /ˈmaʊntənz/
move *v* /muːv/
mushrooms *n pl* /ˈmʌʃruːmz/

never *adv* /ˈnevə(r)/
news *n* /njuːz/
night *n* /naɪt/
noisy *adj* /ˈnɔɪzi/
north-west *adj* /ˈnɔːθ ˌwest/

occasionally *adv* /əˈkeɪʒnəli/
ocean *n* /ˈəʊʃn/
often *adv* /ˈɒftən, ˈɒfn/
one-fifth *n* /ˌwʌn ˈfɪfθ/
order *n* /ˈɔːdə(r)/
origin *n* /ˈɒrədʒɪn/

Pacific (Ocean) *n* /pəˌsɪfɪk ˈəʊʃn/
pasta *n* /ˈpæstə/
peak *n* /piːk/
the Philippines *n pl* /ðə ˈfɪləpiːnz/
play *v* /pleɪ/
pool *n* /puːl/

popular *adj* /ˈpɒpjələ(r)/
possession *n* /pəˈzeʃn/
prefer *v* /prɪˈfɜː(r)/
publisher *n* /ˈpʌblɪʃə(r)/
puddle *n* /ˈpʌdl/
puncture *n* /ˈpʌŋktʃə(r)/

rain *n, v* /reɪn/
rainfall *n* /ˈreɪnfɔːl/
rainy *adj* /ˈreɪni/
reference *n* /ˈrefrəns/
region *n* /ˈriːdʒən/
researcher *n* /rɪˈsɜːtʃə(r)/
result *n* /rɪˈzʌlt/
rotate *v* /rəʊˈteɪt/

the Sahara *n* /ðə səˈhɑːrə/
sand *n* /sænd/
sea *n* /siː/
season *n* /ˈsiːzn/
section *n* /ˈsekʃn/
share *v* /ʃeə(r)/
similar *adj* /ˈsɪmələ(r)/
size *n* /saɪz/
ski *v* /skiː/
sky *n* /skaɪ/
snow *n, v* /snəʊ/
snowy *adj* /ˈsnəʊi/
sometimes *adv* /ˈsʌmtaɪmz/
soup *n* /suːp/
source *n* /sɔːs/
southern *adj* /ˈsʌðən/
sports *n pl* /spɔːts/
spring *n* /sprɪŋ/
statement *n* /ˈsteɪtmənt/
stay *v* /steɪ/
stones *n pl* /stəʊnz/
storm *n* /stɔːm/
strong *adj* /strɒŋ/
study group *n* /ˈstʌdi ˌgruːp/
summer *n* /ˈsʌmə(r)/
summer-house *n* /ˈsʌmə ˌhaʊs/
sun *n* /sʌn/
sunny *adj* /ˈsʌni/
surf *v* /sɜːf/
swim *v* /swɪm/

temperature *n* /ˈtemprətʃə(r)/
tips *n pl* /tɪps/
title *n* /ˈtaɪtl/
track *v* /træk/
trees *n pl* /triːz/
typhoon *n* /taɪˈfuːn/

useful *adj* /ˈjuːsfl/
usually *adv* /ˈjuːʒʊəli/

vegetables *n pl* /ˈvedʒtəblz/
vegetation *n* /ˌvedʒɪˈteɪʃn/
visualize *v* /ˈvɪʒʊəlaɪz/
visuals *n pl* /ˈvɪʒʊəlz/

warm *adj, v* /wɔːm/
warmth *n* /wɔːmθ/
waters *n pl* /ˈwɔːtəz/
waves *n pl* /weɪvz/
weak *adj* /wiːk/
website *n* /ˈwebsaɪt/
wet *adj* /wet/
whole *adj* /həʊl/
wind *n* /wɪnd/
windy *adj* /ˈwɪndi/
winter *n* /ˈwɪntə(r)/
wooden *adj* /ˈwʊdn/
year *n* /jɪə(r)/

Unit 4

air-conditioning *n*
   /ˈeə kənˌdɪʃnɪŋ/
architect *n* /ˈɑːkɪtekt/
bathroom *n* /ˈbɑːθruːm/
beautiful *adj* /ˈbjuːtɪfl/
bedroom *n* /ˈbedruːm/
bottom *n* /ˈbɒtəm/
brick *n* /brɪk/
building material *n*
   /ˈbɪldɪŋ məˌtɪəriəl/

cake *n* /keɪk/
catch fire *v* /ˌkætʃ ˈfaɪə(r)/
charity *n* /ˈtʃærəti/
cheap *adj* /tʃiːp/
climb *v* /klaɪm/
content *n* /ˈkɒntent/
cool *adj* /kuːl/
cut *v* /kʌt/

decorations *n pl* /ˌdekəˈreɪʃnz/
design *v* /dɪˈzaɪn/
diamond *n* /ˈdaɪəmənd/
diary *n* /ˈdaɪəri/
die *v* /daɪ/

easy *adj* /ˈiːzi/
engine *n* /ˈendʒɪn/
expensive *adj* /ɪkˈspensɪv/

famous *adj* /ˈfeɪməs/
first floor *n* /ˌfɜːst ˈflɔː(r)/
floor *n* /flɔː(r)/

gate *n* /geɪt/
glass *n* /glɑːs/
ground floor *n* /ˌgraʊnd ˈflɔː(r)/
growth *n* /grəʊθ/

hard *adj* /hɑːd/
height *n* /haɪt/
holidays *n pl* /ˈhɒlədeɪz/

industry *n* /ˈɪndəstri/
informal *adj* /ɪnˈfɔːml/
Islamic *adj* /ɪzˈlæmɪk/

left *n* /left/
lift *n, v* /lɪft/
light *adj, n* /laɪt/
living room *n* /ˈlɪvɪŋ ˌruːm/
local *adj* /ˈləʊkl/
located *adj* /ləʊˈkeɪtɪd/

marble *n* /ˈmɑːbl/
material *n* /məˈtɪəriəl/
members *n pl* /ˈmembəz/
metres *n pl* /ˈmiːtəz/
middle *n* /ˈmɪdl/
minarets *n pl* /ˌmɪnəˈrets/
modern *adj* /ˈmɒdn/

natural *adj* /ˈnætʃrəl/
nearby *adv* /ˌnɪəˈbaɪ/
north *n* /nɔːθ/

old *adj* /əʊld/

paintings *n pl* /ˈpeɪntɪŋz/
pale *adj* /peɪl/
panoramic *adj* /ˌpænəˈræmɪk/
personal *adj* /ˈpɜːsənl/
platform *n* /ˈplætfɔːm/
poor *adj* /pɔː(r)/
public *n* /ˈpʌblɪk/

put on *v* /ˌpʊt ˈɒn/
really *adv* /ˈriːəli/
rest *n* /rest/
rich *adj* /rɪtʃ/
right *n* /raɪt/
river *n* /ˈrɪvə(r)/
roof *n* /ruːf/

sandstone *n* /ˈsændstəʊn/
second floor *n* /ˌsekənd ˈflɔː(r)/
sick *adj* /sɪk/
sitting room *n* /ˈsɪtɪŋ ˌruːm/
situated *adj* /ˈsɪtʃʊeɪtɪd/
skyscraper *n* /ˈskaɪskreɪpə(r)/
snakes *n pl* /sneɪks/
software *n* /ˈsɒftweə(r)/
south *n* /saʊθ/
staircase *n* /ˈsteəkeɪs/
stairs *n pl* /steəz/
stars *n pl* /stɑːz/
steel *n* /stiːl/
stone *n* /stəʊn/
strength *n* /streŋθ/
style *n* /staɪl/
summary *n* /ˈsʌməri/
Sweden *n* /ˈswiːdn/
Switzerland *n* /ˈswɪtsələnd/
symbolize *v* /ˈsɪmbəlaɪz/

tall *adj* /tɔːl/
tomb *n* /tuːm/
top *n* /tɒp/
tower *n* /ˈtaʊə(r)/

unhealthy *adj* /ʌnˈhelθi/
unusual *adj* /ʌnˈjuːʒʊəl/
upper *adj* /ˈʌpə(r)/

viewing platform *n*
   /ˈvjuːɪŋ ˌplætfɔːm/
visitors *n pl* /ˈvɪzɪtəz/

walls *n pl* /wɔːlz/
world *n* /wɜːld/

Yemen *n* /ˈjemən/

Unit 5

academy *n* /əˈkædəmi/
accounting *n* /əˈkaʊntɪŋ/
administration *n* /ədˌmɪnɪˈstreɪʃn/
admissions *n pl* /ədˈmɪʃnz/
adult *n* /ˈædʌlt/
aerospace *n* /ˈeərəʊspeɪs/
application form *n*
  /ˌæplɪˈkeɪʃn ˌfɔːm/
apply (for) *v* /əˈplaɪ (fə)/
arrows *n pl* /ˈærəʊz/
arts *n pl* /ɑːts/
biological sciences *n pl*
  /ˌbaɪəˌlɒdʒɪkl ˈsaɪənsɪz/
bookshelf *n* /ˈbʊkʃelf/
brochure *n* /ˈbrəʊʃə(r)/
Canada *n* /ˈkænədə/
cause *v* /kɔːz/
certificate *n* /səˈtɪfɪkət/
chairman *n* /ˈtʃeəmən/
chemistry *n* /ˈkemɪstri/
clever *adj* /ˈklevə(r)/
computing *n* /kəmˈpjuːtɪŋ/
concert *n* /ˈkɒnsət/
contrast *n* /ˈkɒntrɑːst/
cook *n* /kʊk/
correctly *adv* /kəˈrektli/
dear *adj* /dɪə(r)/
degree *n* /dɪˈɡriː/
department *n* /dɪˈpɑːtmənt/
details *n pl* /ˈdiːteɪlz/
difficulties *n pl* /ˈdɪfɪkəltiz/
diploma *n* /dɪˈpləʊmə/
disagree *v* /ˌdɪsəˈɡriː/
Dr *n* /ˈdɒktə(r)/
easily *adv* /ˈiːzəli/
economics *n* /ˌiːkəˈnɒmɪks, ˌekə-/
ending *n* /ˈendɪŋ/
environment *n* /ɪnˈvaɪrənmənt/
essay *n* /ˈeseɪ/
especially *adv* /ɪˈspeʃəli/
Europe *n* /ˈjʊərəp/
family name *n* /ˈfæməli ˌneɪm/
fax *n* /fæks/
fluent *adj* /ˈfluːənt/
found *v* /faʊnd/
full-time *adj* /ˈfʊl ˌtaɪm/
genius *n* /ˈdʒiːniəs/
geology *n* /dʒiˈɒlədʒi/
greeting *n* /ˈɡriːtɪŋ/
higher education *n*
  /ˌhaɪər ˌedʒʊˈkeɪʃn/
highlight *v* /ˈhaɪlaɪt/
history *n* /ˈhɪstri/
hobby *n* /ˈhɒbi/
human resources *n pl*
  /ˌhjuːmən rɪˈzɔːsɪz/
intelligent *adj* /ɪnˈtelɪdʒənt/
interest *v* /ˈɪntrəst/
interested *adj* /ˈɪntrəstɪd/
IT *n* /ˌaɪ ˈtiː/
knife *n* /naɪf/
law *n* /lɔː/
lonely *adj* /ˈləʊnli/
look forward to *v*
  /ˌlʊk ˈfɔːwəd tə/

management *n* /ˈmænɪdʒmənt/
margins *n pl* /ˈmɑːdʒɪnz/
maths *n* /mæθs/
mature *adj* /məˈtʃʊə(r)/
mechanics *n* /məˈkænɪks/
medicine *n* /ˈmedsn/
modern languages *n pl*
  /ˌmɒdn ˈlæŋɡwɪdʒɪz/
number *v* /ˈnʌmbə(r)/
officer *n* /ˈɒfɪsə(r)/
online *adv* /ɒnˈlaɪn/
opposite *n* /ˈɒpəzɪt/
overlook *v* /ˌəʊvəˈlʊk/
part-time *adj* /ˈpɑːt ˌtaɪm/
passport *n* /ˈpɑːspɔːt/
physics *n* /ˈfɪzɪks/
pollution *n* /pəˈluːʃn/
population *n* /ˌpɒpjəˈleɪʃn/
postgraduate *n* /ˌpəʊstˈɡrædjuət/
predictions *n pl* /prɪˈdɪkʃnz/
private *adj* /ˈpraɪvət/
recently *adv* /ˈriːsəntli/
Russia *n* /ˈrʌʃə/
schoolteachers *n pl* /ˈskuːlˌtiːtʃəz/
skin cancer *n* /ˈskɪn ˌkænsə(r)/
social sciences *n pl*
  /ˌsəʊʃl ˈsaɪənsɪz/
special *adj* /ˈspeʃl/
sports sciences *n pl*
  /ˈspɔːts ˌsaɪənsɪz/
teenagers *n pl* /ˈtiːneɪdʒəz/
total *adj* /ˈtəʊtl/
UK *n* /ˌjuː ˈkeɪ/
undergraduate *n* /ˌʌndəˈɡrædjuət/
United Kingdom *n*
  /juːˌnaɪtɪd ˈkɪŋdəm/
virus *n* /ˈvaɪrəs/
vitamin D *n* /ˌvɪtəmɪn ˈdiː/
young *adj* /jʌŋ/
Yours faithfully /ˌjɔːz ˈfeɪθfəli/
Yours sincerely /ˌjɔːz sɪnˈsɪəli/
wait *v* /weɪt/
wedding *n* /ˈwedɪŋ/

Unit 6

accurate *adj* /ˈækjərət/
advertisement *n* /ədˈvɜːtɪsmənt/
aeroplane *n* /ˈeərəpleɪn/
artificial *adj* /ˌɑːtɪˈfɪʃl/
at least /ət ˈliːst/
atomic *adj* /əˈtɒmɪk/
available *adj* /əˈveɪləbl/
batteries *n pl* /ˈbætəriz/
bluetooth *n* /ˈbluːtuːθ/
boats *n pl* /bəʊts/
body *n* /ˈbɒdi/
bury *v* /ˈberi/
businessmen *n pl* /ˈbɪznəsmən/
businesswomen *n pl*
  /ˈbɪznəswɪmɪn/
calculate *v* /ˈkælkjəleɪt/
calculator *n* /ˈkælkjəleɪtə(r)/
carpets *n pl* /ˈkɑːpɪts/
circle *v* /ˈsɜːkl/
clause *n* /klɔːz/
clean *v* /kliːn/
clocks *n pl* /klɒks/
common *adj* /ˈkɒmən/
compact discs *n pl*
  /ˌkɒmpækt ˈdɪsks/
construction *n* /kənˈstrʌkʃn/
contact *v* /ˈkɒntækt/
contact lenses *n pl*
  /ˈkɒntækt ˌlenzɪz/
contain *v* /kənˈteɪn/
control *v* /kənˈtrəʊl/
copies *n pl* /ˈkɒpiz/
criminals *n pl* /ˈkrɪmɪnlz/
deal with *v* /ˈdiːl ˌwɪð/
defense *n* US /dɪˈfens/
deployment *n* /dɪˈplɔɪmənt/
device *n* /dɪˈvaɪs/
digital cameras *n pl*
  /ˌdɪdʒɪtl ˈkæmərəz/
dish *n* /dɪʃ/
dishwasher *n* /ˈdɪʃwɒʃə(r)/
distance *n* /ˈdɪstəns/
documents *n pl* /ˈdɒkjəmənts/
DVD player *n*
  /ˌdiː viː ˈdiː ˌpleɪə(r)/
electricity *n* /ɪˌlekˈtrɪsəti/
electronic *adj* /ɪˌlekˈtrɒnɪk/
elephant *n* /ˈelɪfənt/
encyclopaedia *n* /ɪnˌsaɪkləˈpiːdiə/
energy *n* /ˈenədʒi/
exact *adj* /ɪɡˈzækt/
exactly *adv* /ɪɡˈzæktli/
extraction *n* /ɪkˈstrækʃn/
fast *adv* /fɑːst/
fit *v* /fɪt/
fix *v* /fɪks/
four-wheel drive *adj*
  /ˌfɔː ˌwiːl ˈdraɪv/
free *adj* /friː/
generate *v* /ˈdʒenəreɪt/
gold *n* /ɡəʊld/
GPS *n* /ˌdʒiː piː ˈes/
ground station *n* /ˈɡraʊnd ˌsteɪʃn/
group *n* /ɡruːp/
handbags *n pl* /ˈhændbæɡz/

hold *v* /həʊld/
homophones *n pl* /ˈhɒməfəʊnz/
honest *adj* /ˈɒnɪst/
imagine *v* /ɪˈmædʒɪn/
instrument *n* /ˈɪnstrəmənt/
international *adj* /ˌɪntəˈnæʃnəl/
intricacies *n pl* /ˈɪntrɪkəsiz/
invention *n* /ɪnˈvenʃn/
jewellery *n* /ˈdʒuːəlri/
Jupiter *n* /ˈdʒuːpɪtə(r)/
kilograms *n pl* /ˈkɪləɡræmz/
kinetic energy *n* /kɪˌnetɪk ˈenədʒi/
kg *n* /ˌkeɪ ˈdʒiː, ˈkɪləɡræmz/
be known as *v* /bɪ ˈnəʊn əz/
laptop (computer) *n*
  /ˈlæptɒp (kəmˈpjuːtə)/
large-scale *adj* /ˈlɑːdʒ ˌskeɪl/
laser *n* /ˈleɪzə(r)/
last *adj* /lɑːst/
launch *v* /lɔːntʃ/
learners *n pl* /ˈlɜːnəz/
level *n* /ˈlevl/
liquid *n* /ˈlɪkwɪd/
locate *v* /ləʊˈkeɪt/
look like *v* /ˈlʊk ˌlaɪk/
lost *adj* /lɒst/
machine *n* /məˈʃiːn/
main *adj* /meɪn/
mainly *adv* /ˈmeɪnli/
mains electricity *n*
  /ˌmeɪnz ɪˌlekˈtrɪsəti/
make sure *v* /ˌmeɪk ˈʃʊə(r)/
man-made *adj* /ˌmæn ˈmeɪd/
maps *n pl* /mæps/
marks *n pl* /mɑːks/
mechanic *n* /məˈkænɪk/
metal *n* /ˈmetl/
metro *n* /ˈmetrəʊ/
microwave *n* /ˈmaɪkrəweɪv/
military *n* /ˈmɪlətri/
misspell *v* /ˌmɪs ˈspel/
mobile *n* /ˈməʊbaɪl/
moment *n* /ˈməʊmənt/
moon *n* /muːn/
MP3 player *n*
  /ˌem piː ˈθriː ˌpleɪə(r)/
natural *adj* /ˈnætʃərəl/
navigation *n* /ˌnævɪˈɡeɪʃn/
network *n* /ˈnetwɜːk/
notebook computer *n*
  /ˌnəʊtbʊk kəmˈpjuːtə(r)/
object *n* /ˈɒbdʒɪkt/
objective *adj* /əbˈdʒektɪv/
orbit *n, v* /ˈɔːbɪt/
oven *n* /ˈʌvn/
paper clips *n pl* /ˈpeɪpə ˌklɪps/
part (of) *n* /ˈpɑːt (əv)/
pass *v* /pɑːs/
petrol *n* /ˈpetrəl/
photocopier *n* /ˈfəʊtəʊkɒpiə(r)/
plane *n* /pleɪn/
planets *n pl* /ˈplænɪts/
plastic *n* /ˈplæstɪk/
pocket *n* /ˈpɒkɪt/
popular *adj* /ˈpɒpjələ(r)/
portable *adj* /ˈpɔːtəbl/
position *n, v* /pəˈzɪʃn/

printer *n* /ˈprɪntə(r)/
printing press *n* /ˈprɪntɪŋ ˌpres/
process *n* /ˈprəʊses/
provide *v* /prəˈvaɪd/

radio signal *n* /ˈreɪdiəʊ ˌsɪgnəl/
radio waves *n pl* /ˈreɪdiəʊ ˌweɪvz/
receiver *n* /rɪˈsiːvə(r)/
reliable *adj* /rɪˈlaɪəbl/
remote control *n*
    /rɪˌməʊt kənˈtrəʊl/
report *n* /rɪˈpɔːt/
rice *n* /raɪs/
robot *n* /ˈrəʊbɒt/
rockets *n pl* /ˈrɒkɪts/
run (on) *v* /ˈrʌn (ɒn)/

sailors *n pl* /ˈseɪləz/
satellite *n* /ˈsætəlaɪt/
Segway *n* /ˈsegweɪ/
signs *n pl* /saɪnz/
silk *n* /sɪlk/
simple *adj* /ˈsɪmpl/
situation *n* /ˌsɪtʃuˈeɪʃn/
slow *adj* /sləʊ/
solar system *n* /ˈsəʊlə ˌsɪstəm/
sound *v* /saʊnd/
space *n* /speɪs/
speedometer *n* /spiːˈdɒmɪtə(r)/
street *n* /striːt/
system *n* /ˈsɪstəm/

technical *adj* /ˈteknɪkl/
term *n* /tɜːm/
thermometer *n* /θəˈmɒmɪtə(r)/
tin-opener *n* /ˈtɪn ˌəʊpnə(r)/
transmit *v* /trænsˈmɪt/
transport *n* /ˈtrænspɔːt/
travel *v* /ˈtrævl/
travellers *n pl* /ˈtrævələz/
tropical *adj* /ˈtrɒpɪkl/

update *n* /ˈʌpdeɪt/
up-to-date *adj* /ˌʌp tə ˈdeɪt/
use *n* /juːs/
user *n* /ˈjuːzə(r)/

vacuum cleaner *n*
    /ˈvækjuːm ˌkliːnə(r)/

wash *v* /wɒʃ/
washing machine *n*
    /ˈwɒʃɪŋ məˌʃiːn/
watch *n* /wɒtʃ/
water filters *n pl* /ˈwɔːtə ˌfɪltəz/
website *n* /ˈwebsaɪt/
weigh *v* /weɪ/
wind power *n* /ˈwɪnd ˌpaʊə(r)/
wind turbines *n pl*
    /ˈwɪnd ˌtɜːbaɪnz/
World Wide Web *n*
    /ˌwɜːld ˌwaɪd ˈweb/

Unit 7

add *v* /æd/
add up *v* /ˌæd ˈʌp/
air *n* /eə(r)/
apples *n pl* /ˈæplz/
America *n* /əˈmerɪkə/
Arab *adj* /ˈærəb/
Arabian peninsula *n*
    /əˌreɪbiən pəˈnɪnsjələ/
area *n* /ˈeəriə/
argument *n* /ˈɑːgjəmənt/

beans *n pl* /biːnz/
Bedouin *adj* /ˈbeduɪn/
believe *v* /bɪˈliːv/
boil *v* /bɔɪl/
boiling *adj* /ˈbɔɪlɪŋ/
bowl *n* /bəʊl/
bread *n* /bred/
burgers *n pl* /ˈbɜːgəz/

carrots *n pl* /ˈkærəts/
central *adj* /ˈsentrəl/
chart *n* /tʃɑːt/
chocolate *n* /ˈtʃɒklət/
coffee *n* /ˈkɒfi/
coffee pot *n* /ˈkɒfi ˌpɒt/
conclusion *n* /kənˈkluːʒn/
concrete *n* /ˈkɒŋkriːt/
consumer *n* /kənˈsjuːmə(r)/
costs *n pl* /kɒsts/
culture *n* /ˈkʌltʃə(r)/
cupboard *n* /ˈkʌbəd/

daily *adj* /ˈdeɪli/
delicious *adj* /dɪˈlɪʃəs/
disadvantage *n* /ˌdɪsədˈvɑːntɪdʒ/
disagreement *n* /ˌdɪsəˈgriːmənt/
dislike *v* /dɪsˈlaɪk/
distrust *v* /dɪsˈtrʌst/

effects *n pl* /ɪˈfekts/
Egypt *n* /ˈiːdʒɪpt/
enjoyable *adj* /ɪnˈdʒɔɪəbl/
Ethiopia *n* /ˌiːθiˈəʊpiə/
experience *n* /ɪkˈspɪəriəns/
experiment *n* /ɪkˈsperɪmənt/

far *adj* /fɑː(r)/
farmer *n* /ˈfɑːmə(r)/
Farsi *n* /ˈfɑːsi/
field *n* /fiːld/
first of all /ˌfɜːst əv ˈɔːl/
flour *n* /ˈflaʊə(r)/
fluently *adv* /ˈfluːəntli/
food *n* /fuːd/
food mile *n* /ˈfuːd ˌmaɪl/
foreign *adj* /ˈfɒrən/
fresh *adj* /freʃ/
fridge *n* /frɪdʒ/
friendly *adj* /ˈfrendli/
fruit *n* /fruːt/

global warming *n*
    /ˌgləʊbl ˈwɔːmɪŋ/
grams *n pl* /græmz/
grind *v* /graɪnd/
grains *n pl* /greɪnz/

hard *adv* /hɑːd/
heat *v* /hiːt/
hosts *n pl* /həʊsts/
ice-cream *n* /ˌaɪs ˈkriːm/

impatient *adj* /ɪmˈpeɪʃnt/
import *v* /ɪmˈpɔːt/
imported *adj* /ɪmˈpɔːtɪd/
impossible *adj* /ɪmˈpɒsəbl/
in addition /ˌɪn əˈdɪʃn/
incomplete *adj* /ˌɪnkəmˈpliːt/
increase *v* /ɪnˈkriːs/
ingredients *n pl* /ɪnˈgriːdiənts/
in season /ˌɪn ˈsiːzn/
irregular *adj* /ɪˈregjələ(r)/
irresponsible *adj* /ˌɪrɪˈspɒnsəbl/
Italian *adj* /ɪˈtæliən/
Italy *n* /ˈɪtəli/
items *n pl* /ˈaɪtəmz/

journey *n* /ˈdʒɜːni/
jumbled *adj* /ˈdʒʌmbld/

Kenya *n* /ˈkenjə/

lamb *n* /læm/
land *v* /lænd/
leaves *n pl* /liːvz/
Lebanese *adj* /ˌlebəˈniːz/
lecturer *n* /ˈlektʃərə(r)/
literature *n* /ˈlɪtrətʃə(r)/
loaf *n* /ləʊf/
locally *adv* /ˈləʊkəli/

Malaysia *n* /məˈleɪzə/
market *n* /ˈmɑːkɪt/
miles *n pl* /maɪlz/
mint *n* /mɪnt/
mint tea *n* /ˌmɪnt ˈtiː/
minutes *n pl* /ˈmɪnɪts/
Moroccan *adj* /məˈrɒkən/
Morocco *n* /məˈrɒkəʊ/
music *n* /ˈmjuːzɪk/

New Zealand *n* /ˌnjuː ˈziːlənd/
noise *n* /nɔɪz/
nowadays *adv* /ˈnaʊədeɪz/

omelette *n* /ˈɒmlət/
onions *n pl* /ˈʌnjənz/
opinion *n* /əˈpɪnjən/
originally *adv* /əˈrɪdʒənəli/
origins *n pl* /ˈɒrədʒɪnz/

pasta *n* /ˈpæstə/
pick *v* /pɪk/
pizza *n* /ˈpiːtsə/
plate *n* /pleɪt/
potatoes *n pl* /pəˈteɪtəʊz/
pour *v* /pɔː(r)/
probably *adv* /ˈprɒbəbli/
produce *v* /prəˈdjuːs/
producers *n pl* /prəˈdjuːsəz/
projects *n pl* /ˈprɒdʒekts/

reduce *v* /rɪˈdjuːs/
repair *v* /rɪˈpeə(r)/
require *v* /rɪˈkwaɪə(r)/
rice *n* /raɪs/
roast *v* /rəʊst/
roasted *adj* /ˈrəʊstɪd/

salt *n* /sɔːlt, sɒlt/
sell *v* /sel/
sensible *adj* /ˈsensəbl/
separate *v* /ˈsepəreɪt/
serve *v* /sɜːv/
ships *n pl* /ʃɪps/
sides *n pl* /saɪdz/
signal *n* /ˈsɪgnəl/

similar *adj* /ˈsɪmələ(r)/
similarly *adv* /ˈsɪmələli/
society *n* /səˈsaɪəti/
Spanish *adj* /ˈspænɪʃ/
spread *v* /spred/
store *v* /stɔː(r)/
strawberries *n pl* /ˈstrɔːbəriz/
sugar *n* /ˈʃʊgə(r)/
supermarket *n* /ˈsuːpəmɑːkɪt/
surprised *adj* /səˈpraɪzd/

take off *v* /ˌteɪk ˈɒf/
taste *n* /teɪst/
tasteless *adj* /ˈteɪstləs/
tasty *adj* /ˈteɪsti/
tea *n* /tiː/
teapot *n* /ˈtiːpɒt/
technology *n* /tekˈnɒlədʒi/
tennis *n* /ˈtenɪs/
thousands *n pl* /ˈθaʊzəndz/
tomatoes *n pl* /təˈmɑːtəʊz/
total *n* /ˈtəʊtl/
trade *n* /treɪd/
traditional *adj* /trəˈdɪʃənl/
traditionally *adv* /trəˈdɪʃənəli/
tray *n* /treɪ/
Turkish *n* /ˈtɜːkɪʃ/

UAE *n* /ˌjuː eɪ ˈiː/
unhappy *adj* /ʌnˈhæpi/
unhelpful *adj* /ʌnˈhelpfl/
United Arab Emirates *n*
    /juːˌnaɪtɪd ˌærəb ˈemɪrəts/
unpleasant *adj* /ʌnˈpleznt/
upset *adj* /ʌpˈset/
Urdu *n* /ˈɜːduː/

way of life *n* /ˌweɪ əv ˈlaɪf/
welcoming *adj* /ˈwelkəmɪŋ/
western *adj* /ˈwestən/
wood *adj* /wʊd/
worrying *adj* /ˈwʌriɪŋ/

Unit 8

African *adj* /ˈæfrɪkən/
artists' *n pl* /ˈɑːtɪsts/
Asia *n* /ˈeɪʒə/
Asian *adj* /ˈeɪʒn/
Austria *n* /ˈɒstriə/
Bangladesh *n* /ˌbæŋɡləˈdeʃ/
bar chart *n* /ˈbɑː ˌtʃɑːt/
beach *n* /biːtʃ/
best *adj* /best/
best-known *adj* /ˈbest ˌnəʊn/
births *n pl* /bɜːθs/
birth rate *n* /ˈbɜːθ ˌreɪt/
boating *n* /ˈbəʊtɪŋ/
border *n* /ˈbɔːdə(r)/
Canada *n* /ˈkænədə/
captain *n* /ˈkæptɪn/
census *n* /ˈsensəs/
chains *n pl* /tʃeɪnz/
coast *n* /kəʊst/
commercial *adj* /kəˈmɜːʃl/
cool *adj* /kuːl/
corner *n* /ˈkɔːnə(r)/
cosmopolitan *adj* /ˌkɒzməˈpɒlɪtən/
cover *v* /ˈkʌvə(r)/
crime *n* /kraɪm/
cycling *n* /ˈsaɪklɪŋ/
data *n* /ˈdeɪtə/
disorganized *adj* /dɪsˈɔːɡənaɪzd/
ethnic *adj* /ˈeθnɪk/
ethnically *adv* /ˈeθnɪkli/
facilities *n pl* /fəˈsɪlətiz/
factors *n pl* /ˈfæktəz/
facts *n pl* /fækts/
fashion *n* /ˈfæʃn/
figures *n pl* /ˈfɪɡəz/
Filipinos *n pl* /ˌfɪləˈpiːnəʊz/
forests *n pl* /ˈfɒrɪsts/
graph *n* /ɡrɑːf/
half *n* /hɑːf/
harbour *n* /ˈhɑːbə(r)/
high fashion *n* /ˌhaɪ ˈfæʃn/
high-ranking *adj* /ˈhaɪ ˌræŋkɪŋ/
hiking *n* /ˈhaɪkɪŋ/
historic *adj* /hɪˈstɒrɪk/
include *v* /ɪnˈkluːd/
Indians *n pl* /ˈɪndiənz/
intelligence *n* /ɪnˈtelɪdʒəns/
Iran *n* /ɪˈrɑːn, ɪˈræn/
Japanese *adj* /ˌdʒæpəˈniːz/
Jordan *n* /ˈdʒɔːdn/
Kuwait *n* /kʊˈweɪt/
lie *v* /laɪ/
liveable *adj* /ˈlɪvəbl/
living conditions *n pl* /ˈlɪvɪŋ kənˌdɪʃnz/
low *adj* /ləʊ/
maximum *adj* /ˈmæksɪməm/
mild *adj* /maɪld/
million *n* /ˈmɪljən/
mixed *adj* /mɪkst/
monsoon *n* /mɒnˈsuːn/
mother tongue *n* /ˈmʌðə ˌtʌŋ/
museum *n* /mjuˈziːəm/
naval *adj* /ˈneɪvl/
Nigeria *n* /naɪˈdʒɪəriə/
order *n* /ˈɔːdə(r)/
Pakistan *n* /ˌpækɪˈstɑːn/
panoramic *adj* /ˌpænəˈræmɪk/
Papua New Guinea *n* /ˌpæpjʊə ˌnjuː ˈɡɪni/
peninsula *n* /pəˈnɪnsjələ/
per *prep* /pɜː(r)/
pie chart *n* /ˈpaɪ ˌtʃɑːt/
political *adj* /pəˈlɪtɪkl/
port *n* /pɔːt/
precipitation *n* /prɪˌsɪpɪˈteɪʃn/
quarter *n* /ˈkwɔːtə(r)/
rank *v* /ræŋk/
rarely *adv* /ˈreəli/
rate *n* /reɪt/
recreation *n* /ˌrekriˈeɪʃn/
recreational *adj* /ˌrekriˈeɪʃənl/
rename *v* /ˌriːˈneɪm/
retake *v* /ˌriːˈteɪk/
rise *v* /raɪz/
safety *n* /ˈseɪfti/
scenery *n* /ˈsiːnəri/
scores *n pl* /skɔːz/
second language *n* /ˌsekənd ˈlæŋɡwɪdʒ/
settlement *n* /ˈsetlmənt/
shopping *n* /ˈʃɒpɪŋ/
sights *n pl* /saɪts/
skiing *n* /ˈskiːɪŋ/
snow-capped *adj* /ˈsnəʊ ˌkæpt/
south-west *adj* /ˈsaʊθ ˌwest/
square *n* /skweə(r)/
stadium *n* /ˈsteɪdiəm/
statistics *n pl* /stəˈtɪstɪks/
successful *adj* /səkˈsesfl/
surround *v* /səˈraʊnd/
survey *n* /ˈsɜːveɪ/
Switzerland *n* /ˈswɪtsələnd/
studios *n pl* /ˈstjuːdiəʊz/
table *n* /ˈteɪbl/
top *adj* /tɒp/
tourist centre *n* /ˈtʊərɪst ˌsentə(r)/
trading *n* /ˈtreɪdɪŋ/
trip *n* /trɪp/
unit *n* /ˈjuːnɪt/
United States *n* /juˌnaɪtɪd ˈsteɪts/
Vietnamese *n pl* /ˌvjetnəˈmiːz/
view *n* /vjuː/
visuals *n pl* /ˈvɪʒuəlz/
wood *n* /wʊd/
worst *adj* /wɜːst/
worth *adj* /wɜːθ/

Unit 9

active *adj* /ˈæktɪv/
activity *n* /ækˈtɪvəti/
aims *n pl* /eɪmz/
arm *n* /ɑːm/
articles *n pl* /ˈɑːtɪklz/
average *adj* /ˈævərɪdʒ/
avoid *v* /əˈvɔɪd/
bath *n* /bɑːθ/
bedtime *n* /ˈbedtaɪm/
beneficial *adj* /ˌbenɪˈfɪʃl/
billion *n* /ˈbɪljən/
blood *n* /blʌd/
body *n* /ˈbɒdi/
bone *n* /bəʊn/
brain *n* /breɪn/
brainpower *n* /ˈbreɪnpaʊə(r)/
caffeine *n* /ˈkæfiːn/
cat *n* /kæt/
cells *n pl* /selz/
central nervous system *n* /ˌsentrəl ˈnɜːvəs ˌsɪstəm/
chest *n* /tʃest/
chimpanzee *n* /ˌtʃɪmpænˈziː/
cholesterol *n* /kəˈlestərɒl/
choline *n* /ˈkəʊliːn/
clubs *n pl* /klʌbz/
comfortable *adj* /ˈkʌmftəbl/
compare *v* /kəmˈpeə(r)/
comprehension *n* /ˌkɒmprɪˈhenʃn/
consist of *v* /kənˈsɪst əv/
contents *n pl* /ˈkɒntents/
corporation *n* /ˌkɔːpəˈreɪʃn/
cover *n* /ˈkʌvə(r)/
cow *n* /kaʊ/
create *v* /kriˈeɪt/
cricket *n* /ˈkrɪkɪt/
cyclists *n pl* /ˈsaɪklɪsts/
damage *v* /ˈdæmɪdʒ/
dancing *n* /ˈdɑːnsɪŋ/
dark *adj* /dɑːk/
delicate *adj* /ˈdelɪkət/
diet *n* /ˈdaɪət/
disease *n* /dɪˈziːz/
display *v* /dɪˈspleɪ/
disturb *v* /dɪˈstɜːb/
dolphin *n* /ˈdɒlfɪn/
ear *n* /ɪə(r)/
eggs *n pl* /egz/
emotion *n* /ɪˈməʊʃn/
encourage *v* /ɪnˈkʌrɪdʒ/
exercise *n, v* /ˈeksəsaɪz/
experts *n pl* /ˈekspɜːts/
eye *n* /aɪ/
facts *n pl* /fækts/
fat *n* /fæt/
fatty *adj* /ˈfæti/
fish *n* /fɪʃ/
flow *n* /fləʊ/
foot *n* /fʊt/
functions *n pl* /ˈfʌŋkʃnz/
great *adj* /ɡreɪt/
gym *n* /dʒɪm/
hair *n* /heə(r)/
hand *n* /hænd/
head *n* /hed/
heavy *adj* /ˈhevi/
heart *n* /hɑːt/
human *adj, n* /ˈhjuːmən/
ill *adj* /ɪl/
immune system *n* /ɪˈmjuːn ˌsɪstəm/
importance *n* /ɪmˈpɔːtəns/
improve *v* /ɪmˈpruːv/
index *n* /ˈɪndeks/
in good shape *n* /ɪn ˌɡʊd ˈʃeɪp/
join *v* /dʒɔɪn/
kilos *n pl* /ˈkiːləʊz/
lawyer *n* /ˈlɔːjə(r)/
leader *n* /ˈliːdə(r)/
leg *n* /leɡ/
liver *n* /ˈlɪvə(r)/
lungs *n pl* /lʌŋz/
male *adj* /meɪl/
mathematician *n* /ˌmæθəməˈtɪʃn/
mattress *n* /ˈmætrəs/
memory *n* /ˈmeməri/
mentally *adv* /ˈmentəli/
mention *v* /ˈmenʃn/
midday *n* /mɪdˈdeɪ/
mix *v* /mɪks/
mouth *n* /maʊθ/
neck *n* /nek/
nerve cells *n pl* /ˈnɜːv ˌselz/
neurons *n pl* /ˈnjʊərɒnz/
new *adj* /njuː/
normal *adj* /ˈnɔːml/
nose *n* /nəʊz/
nutrient *n* /ˈnjuːtriənt/
nutritious *adj* /njuˈtrɪʃəs/
nuts *n pl* /nʌts/
organ *n* /ˈɔːɡən/
physical *adj* /ˈfɪzɪkl/
pillows *n pl* /ˈpɪləʊz/
players *n pl* /ˈpleɪəz/
plenty *n* /ˈplenti/
poster *n* /ˈpəʊstə(r)/
print *v* /prɪnt/
program *v* /ˈprəʊɡræm/
protect *v* /prəˈtekt/
puzzles *n pl* /ˈpʌzlz/
recommend *v* /ˌrekəˈmend/
red meat *n* /ˌred ˈmiːt/
relaxed *adj* /rɪˈlækst/
relaxing *adj* /rɪˈlæksɪŋ/
responsible *adj* /rɪˈspɒnsəbl/
revision *n* /rɪˈvɪʒn/
ribs *n pl* /rɪbz/
rock climbers *n pl* /ˈrɒk ˌklaɪməz/
routine *n* /ruːˈtiːn/
self-defence *n* /ˌself dɪˈfens/
sharp *adj* /ʃɑːp/
skin *n* /skɪn/
skull *n* /skʌl/
smoking *n* /ˈsməʊkɪŋ/
skills *n pl* /skɪlz/
sleep *n* /sliːp/
social *adj* /ˈsəʊʃl/
socialize *v* /ˈsəʊʃəlaɪz/
socially *adv* /ˈsəʊʃəli/

solve *v* /sɒlv/
spine *n* /spaɪn/
steps *n pl* /steps/
stomach *n* /'stʌmək/
store *v* /stɔ:(r)/
suggest *v* /sə'dʒest/
summary *n* /'sʌməri/
supper *n* /'sʌpə(r)/
synonym *n* /'sɪnənɪm/
teeth *n pl* /ti:θ/
Theory of Relativity *n*
  /ˌθɪəri əv ˌrelə'tɪvəti/
thinking *n* /'θɪŋkɪŋ/
tips *n pl* /tɪps/
tired *adj* /'taɪəd/
title page *n* /'taɪtl ˌpeɪdʒ/
unusual *adj* /ʌn'ju:ʒʊəl/
waist *n* /weɪst/
weight *n* /weɪt/
work-outs *n pl* /'wɜ:k ˌaʊts/
world famous *adj* /ˌwɜ:ld 'feɪməs/
wide *adj* /waɪd/

Unit 10

according to *prep* /ə'kɔ:dɪŋ tə/
advantages *n pl* /əd'va:ntɪdʒɪz/
aerobics *n* /eə'rəʊbɪks/
airline *n* /'eəlaɪn/
alive *adj* /ə'laɪv/
also *adv* /'ɔ:lsəʊ/
the Americas *n pl* /ði ə'merɪkəz/
antonym *n* /'æntənɪm/
approve *v* /ə'pru:v/
arrive *v* /ə'raɪv/
as a result /əz ə rɪ'zʌlt/
average *n* /'ævərɪdʒ/

bar chart *n* /'ba: ˌtʃa:t/
barrel *n* /'bærəl/
birth *n* /bɜ:θ/
blood pressure *n* /'blʌd ˌpreʃə(r)/
book *v* /bʊk/
boss *n* /bɒs/
Botswana *n* /bɒt'swa:nə/
boxing *n* /'bɒksɪŋ/

calculations *n pl* /ˌkælkjə'leɪʃnz/
cancer *n* /'kænsə(r)/
Caribbean *n* /ˌkærə'bi:ən/
charts *n pl* /tʃa:ts/
cholesterol *n* /kə'lestərɒl/
clean *adj* /kli:n/
competition *n* /ˌkɒmpə'tɪʃn/
conference *n* /'kɒnfərəns/
crash *n* /kræʃ/
cure *n* /kjʊə(r)/
cycle *v* /'saɪkl/

danger *n* /'deɪndʒə(r)/
death *n* /deθ/
decimals *n pl* /'desɪmlz/
decline *v* /dɪ'klaɪn/
decrease *v* /dɪ'kri:s/
depart *v* /dɪ'pa:t/
develop *v* /dɪ'veləp/
developed *adj* /dɪ'veləpt/
developing *adj* /dɪ'veləpɪŋ/
diabetes *n* /ˌdaɪə'bi:ti:z/
dirty *adj* /'dɜ:ti/
disapprove *v* /ˌdɪsə'pru:v/
disorganized *adj* /dɪs'ɔ:gənaɪzd/
drugs *n pl* /drʌgz/
dull *adj* /dʌl/

Eastern Mediterranean *n*
  /ˌi:stən ˌmedɪtə'reɪnɪən/
expect *v* /ɪk'spekt/

failure *n* /'feɪljə(r)/
fall *v* /fɔ:l/
fast *adj* /fa:st/
fast food *n* /ˌfa:st 'fu:d/
females *n pl* /'fi:meɪlz/
figure *n* /'fɪgə(r)/

Germany *n* /'dʒɜ:məni/
go down *v* /ˌgəʊ 'daʊn/
go into business *v*
  /ˌgəʊ ˌɪntə 'bɪznəs/
go up *v* /ˌgəʊ 'ʌp/
graphs *n pl* /gra:fs/
growing *adj* /'grəʊɪŋ/

health care *n* /'helθ ˌkeə(r)/
heart disease *n* /'ha:t dɪˌzi:z/
high *adj* /haɪ/

ideal *adj* /aɪ'di:əl/
illegal *adj* /ɪ'li:gl/
impersonal *adj* /ˌɪm'pɜ:sənl/
increase *n, v* /'ɪŋkri:s, ɪn'kri:s/
indicate *v* /'ɪndɪkeɪt/
inexpensive *adj* /ˌɪnɪk'spensɪv/
inhabitants *n pl* /ɪn'hæbɪtənts/
injure *v* /'ɪndʒə(r)/
instead *adv* /ɪn'sted/

jog *v* /dʒɒg/

lack *n* /læk/
large *adj* /la:dʒ/
Latin America *n* /ˌlætɪn ə'merɪkə/
lecturer *n* /'lektʃərə(r)/
legal *adj* /'li:gl/
life *n* /laɪf/
life expectancy *n* /'laɪf
  ɪkˌspektənsi/
lifestyles *n pl* /'laɪfstaɪlz/
lose weight *v* /ˌlu:z 'weɪt/
low *adj* /ləʊ/

malaria *n* /mə'leərɪə/
males *n pl* /meɪlz/
mountains *n pl* /'maʊntənz/

Near East *n* /ˌnɪər 'i:st/
nervous *adj* /'nɜ:vəs/
North America *n* /ˌnɔ:θ ə'merɪkə/

occur *v* /ə'kɜ:(r)/
on the other hand
  /ˌɒn ði 'ʌðə ˌhænd/
ordinal numbers *n pl*
  /'ɔ:dɪnl ˌnʌmbəz/
organized *adj* /'ɔ:gənaɪzd/
overweight *adj* /ˌəʊvə'weɪt/

per *prep* /pɜ:(r)/
percentage *n* /pə'sentɪdʒ/
personal *adj* /'pɜ:sənl/
Peru *n* /pə'ru:/
photocopier *n* /'fəʊtəʊkɒpɪə(r)/
picnics *n pl* /'pɪknɪks/
politicians *n pl* /ˌpɒlə'tɪʃnz/
poor *adj* /pɔ:(r)/
possible *adj* /'pɒsəbl/
prepare *v* /prɪ'peə(r)/
processed *adj* /'prəʊsest/
proper *adj* /'prɒpə(r)/
proportion *n* /prə'pɔ:ʃn/
purchase *v* /'pɜ:tʃəs/

rate *n* /reɪt/
reader *n* /'ri:də(r)/
reduce *v* /rɪ'dju:s/
refer *v* /rɪ'fɜ:(r)/
regularly *adv* /'regjələli/
rise *v* /raɪz/

serious *adj* /'sɪərɪəs/
show *v* /ʃəʊ/
skimmed milk *n* /ˌskɪmd 'mɪlk/
South-East Asia *n*
  /ˌsaʊθ i:st 'eɪʒə/
spread *n* /spred/
statistics *n pl* /stə'tɪstɪks/
stress *n* /stres/
success *n* /sək'ses/
suffer from *v* /'sʌfə ˌfrɒm, frəm/
synonym *n* /'sɪnənɪm/

table *n* /'teɪbl/

the Taj Mahal *n*
  /ðə ˌta:dʒ mə'ha:l/
tickets *n pl* /'tɪkɪts/
uninteresting *adj* /ʌn'ɪntrəstɪŋ/
wealthy *adj* /'welθi/
weight *n* /weɪt/
Western Pacific *n*
  /ˌwestən pə'sɪfɪk/
WHO *n* /ˌdʌblju: eɪtʃ 'əʊ/
World Health Organization *n*
  /ˌwɜ:ld 'helθ ˌɔ:gənaɪˌzeɪʃn/
worldwide *adv* /ˌwɜ:ld'waɪd/

PHONETIC SYMBOLS

Consonants

1	/p/	as in	**pen**	/pen/
2	/b/	as in	**big**	/bɪg/
3	/t/	as in	**tea**	/tiː/
4	/d/	as in	**do**	/duː/
5	/k/	as in	**cat**	/kæt/
6	/g/	as in	**go**	/gəʊ/
7	/f/	as in	**four**	/fɔː/
8	/v/	as in	**very**	/ˈveri/
9	/s/	as in	**son**	/sʌn/
10	/z/	as in	**zoo**	/zuː/
11	/l/	as in	**live**	/lɪv/
12	/m/	as in	**my**	/maɪ/
13	/n/	as in	**near**	/nɪə/
14	/h/	as in	**happy**	/ˈhæpi/
15	/r/	as in	**red**	/red/
16	/j/	as in	**yes**	/jes/
17	/w/	as in	**want**	/wɒnt/
18	/θ/	as in	**thanks**	/θæŋks/
19	/ð/	as in	**the**	/ðə/
20	/ʃ/	as in	**she**	/ʃiː/
21	/ʒ/	as in	**television**	/ˈtelɪvɪʒn/
22	/tʃ/	as in	**child**	/tʃaɪld/
23	/dʒ/	as in	**German**	/ˈdʒɜːmən/
24	/ŋ/	as in	**English**	/ˈɪŋglɪʃ/

Vowels

25	/iː/	as in	**see**	/siː/
26	/ɪ/	as in	**his**	/hɪz/
27	/i/	as in	**twenty**	/ˈtwenti/
28	/e/	as in	**ten**	/ten/
29	/æ/	as in	**stamp**	/stæmp/
30	/ɑː/	as in	**father**	/ˈfɑːðə/
31	/ɒ/	as in	**hot**	/hɒt/
32	/ɔː/	as in	**morning**	/ˈmɔːnɪŋ/
33	/ʊ/	as in	**football**	/ˈfʊtbɔːl/
34	/uː/	as in	**you**	/juː/
35	/ʌ/	as in	**sun**	/sʌn/
36	/ɜː/	as in	**learn**	/lɜːn/
37	/ə/	as in	**letter**	/ˈletə/

Diphthongs (two vowels together)

38	/eɪ/	as in	**name**	/neɪm/
39	/əʊ/	as in	**no**	/nəʊ/
40	/aɪ/	as in	**my**	/maɪ/
41	/aʊ/	as in	**how**	/haʊ/
42	/ɔɪ/	as in	**boy**	/bɔɪ/
43	/ɪə/	as in	**hear**	/hɪə/
44	/eə/	as in	**where**	/weə/
45	/ʊə/	as in	**tour**	/tʊə/

OXFORD
UNIVERSITY PRESS

Great Clarendon Street, Oxford OX2 6DP

Oxford University Press is a department of the University of Oxford.
It furthers the University's objective of excellence in research, scholarship,
and education by publishing worldwide in

Oxford New York

Auckland Cape Town Dar es Salaam Hong Kong Karachi
Kuala Lumpur Madrid Melbourne Mexico City Nairobi
New Delhi Shanghai Taipei Toronto

With offices in

Argentina Austria Brazil Chile Czech Republic France Greece
Guatemala Hungary Italy Japan Poland Portugal Singapore
South Korea Switzerland Thailand Turkey Ukraine Vietnam

OXFORD and OXFORD ENGLISH are registered trade marks of
Oxford University Press in the UK and in certain other countries

© Oxford University Press 2006

ACKNOWLEDGEMENTS

Illustrations by: Kathy Baxendale p12 (neat handwriting), 20 (diagrams); Jason Cook p 27; Mark Duffin pp 21, 23, 35 (diagram of GPS & satellites in orbit), 41 (map); Andy Hammond p5; Joe Morse/The Artworks p54; Oxford Designers & Illustrators p57

Commissioned photography by: Pearl Bevan, p5, p33; Ellie Farr p31

We would also like to thank the following for permission to reproduce the following photographs: Alamy Images pp11 (Young woman holding flowers/Bloom Works Inc.), 11 (man on bike in gym/Scott Hortop), 11 (Fireman fighting fire/Dinodia Images), 18 (Traditional Russian dachas,Russia/Iain Masterton), 22 (Hong Kong China/BL Images Ltd), 24 (Bilderbox/INSADCO Photography), 28 (Cambridge Massachusetts, USA/Andre Jenny), 28 (Christ Church College, Oxford/Julie Woodhouse), 29 (Oxfordshire Oxford/PCL), 34 (mini cooper sports car/Alan King), 34 (Airbus A380/Antony Nettle), 34 (Computer/D. Hurst), 34 (Unbranded digital radio/Joe Tree), 34 (Label Printing Press Boras Sweden/Danita Delimont), 34 (Big screen TV/Judith Collins), 34 (washing machine/Hugh Threlfall), 35 (Mobile Phone/Rodolfo Arpia), 36 (mp3 music player/D. Hurst), 36 (photocopier/Ingram Publishing), 36 (remote control/graficart.net), 39 (Train platform Moorgate underground station London UK/Photofusion Picture Library), 41 (tomatoes on truck/Mark Gibson), 43 (Mint tea Morocco/Simon Reddy), 45 (woman separating skins from coffee beans/Contact), 45 (Coffee pot coffee beans and cup of coffee on a saucer/Nordicphotos), 45 (Arabic coffee pot/Malcolm Park), 47 (Vancouver British Columbia Canada/Lucidio Studio, Inc.), 49 (Mumbai/Travel Ink), 50 (Hong Kong China/Jon Arnold Images), 55 (ImageState/Sleep), 59 (Knickerbocker Glory/Ingram Publishing); Corbis pp4 (Young Man Reading in Windowsill/zefa/A. Inden), 9 (Young Man Leaning Back/JLP/Jose Luis Pelaez), 37 (Woman Using a Laptop On Safari/Strauss/Curtis), 59 (Children running/Tom & Dee Ann McCarthy); Getty Images pp6 (Arab Lady/Gulfimages/Pankaj & Insy Shah), 11 (Angry taxi driver/ Altrendo), 25 (Rock Palace/Lonely Planet Images/Chris Mellor), 28 (Russia/Stone/John Lamb), 38 (Wind Farm/PhotonicaSilvia Otte/), 42 (Pasta/StockFood Creative), 53 (Stylised brain and CNS/3D4Medical.com), 53 (Pain/Taxi/Michael Freeman), 61 (Male Mosquito Hatching /Science Faction/Hans Pfletschinger); Impact Photos Ltd pp16 (Korkerboom Quiver Tree, Namibia, Africa/Thierry Bouzac), 16 (A cyclist in the snow /Christophe Bluntzer); OUP p51 (Frankfurt skyline, Germany/ Imagesource); Pictures Colour Library Ltd p22 (Agra, Taj Mahal/Adrian Pope); PunchStock pp6 (business man smiling/image100), 13 (Student with text book/Design Pics), 15 (Portrait of Businessman at Harbor/Corbis), 17 (Cyclone/Goodshot), 18 (Death Valley, Mesquite Dunes, California, USA/Photographer's Choice), 20 (Volcano, Chile/ImageSource), 34 (website/Goodshot), 34 (telephone/Stockdisc), 34 (Satellite/Photodisc), 36 (Electric drill), 36 (Close up of a speedometer/Stockdisc), 37 (Illustration of a Comet Orbiting a Red Planet/Photodisc), 38 (Windmill/Photodisc), 59 (diabetes equipment/Stockdisc); Science Photo Library p16 (Hurricane/Jim Reed); Telegraph Colour Library/K&K Ammann p56.

The authors and publisher are grateful to those who have given permission to reproduce the following extracts and adaptations of copyright material: p8, p14, 26 entries from the *Oxford Essential Dictionary* © Oxford University Press 2006. Reproduced by kind permission. p38 Extract from *The Illustrated History of Wind Power Development* by Darrell M Dodge. Reproduced by permission of Darrell M Dodge; p56 Extracts from *Complete Biology* by WR Pickering. Reproduced by permission of Oxford University Press.